Manatee/Humanity

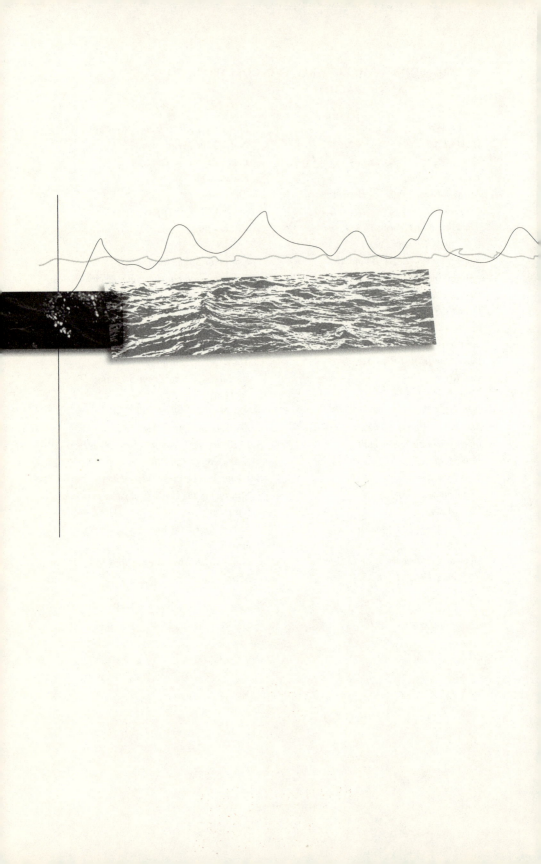

Manatee/Humanity

A N N E   W A L D M A N

P E N G U I N   P O E T S

PENGUIN BOOKS

Published by the Penguin Group

Penguin Group (USA) Inc., 375 Hudson Street, New York, New York 10014, U.S.A.
Penguin Group (Canada), 90 Eglinton Avenue East, Suite 700, Toronto, Ontario, Canada M4P 2Y3
(a division of Pearson Penguin Canada Inc.)
Penguin Books Ltd, 80 Strand, London WC2R 0RL, England
Penguin Ireland, 25 St Stephen's Green, Dublin 2, Ireland (a division of Penguin Books Ltd)
Penguin Group (Australia), 250 Camberwell Road, Camberwell, Victoria 3124, Australia
(a division of Pearson Australia Group Pty Ltd)
Penguin Books India Pvt Ltd, 11 Community Centre, Panchsheel Park, New Delhi–110 017, India
Penguin Group (NZ), 67 Apollo Drive, Rosedale, North Shore 0632, New Zealand
(a division of Pearson New Zealand Ltd)
Penguin Books (South Africa) (Pty) Ltd, 24 Sturdee Avenue, Rosebank, Johannesburg 2196,
South Africa

Penguin Books Ltd, Registered Offices:
80 Strand, London WC2R 0RL, England

First published in Penguin Books 2009

1   3   5   7   9   10   8   6   4   2

Acknowledgments to the original publishers of selections in this book appear on page x.

LIBRARY OF CONGRESS CATALOGING IN PUBLICATION DATA
Waldman, Anne, 1945–
Manatee-humanity / Anne Waldman.
p. cm.—(Penguin poets)
ISBN 978-0-14-311521-2
I. Title.
PS3573.A4215M35   2009
811'.54—dc22   2009003689

Printed in the United States of America
Set in Bembo
Designed by Ginger Legato

Was living: panting like a frighted wolf, and howling

—WILLIAM BLAKE

Effort lay in us
before religion
at pond bottom

—LORINE NIEDECKER

"Lirgga songs . . . are received by the mermaid Dreamings who live in Billabongs . . ."

—ALLAN MARETT (*The Wanga of North Australia*)

Out and starts the mermaiden,
Wi a fan into her hand:
"Keep up your hearts, my merry men',
For ye're near the dry land."
Out and spak Earl Patrick Graham,
Wi the saut tear in his ee:
"Now sin we've seen the mermaiden,
Dry land we'll never see."

—VARIANT, SIR PATRICK SPENS

stealth bombers ghosts shrouds
Tibetan journeyings spaces of time between magnets & continents
causeways into another continuum

—KAMAU BRATHWAITE

the manatee is found in slow-moving rivers
the manatee moves in estuaries, moves in saltwater bays

A C K N O W L E D G M E N T S

American Poetry Review, Shivastan Press, *XCP: CrossCultural Poetics, The Brooklyn Rail,* Farfalla, McMillan & Parrish, Longhouse, Ambrose Bye and Fast Speaking Music's "The Eye of the Falcon" and "Matching Half," and the perspicuity and friendship of Mei-mei Berssenbrugge. Gratitude to the Bellagio Study and Conference Center and its denizens where the written manatee first had life among neuroscientists, scholars, and writers: Sam Wang, Sandra Aamodt, Kenneth Britten, Stephen Barber, Seemin Qayum, Sinclair Thomson and Bishaka Datta. And to Douglas Dunn for dancing the manatee. And always deep bows to the Buddhist elders and teachers. *Sarva mangalam.*

CONTENTS

{undercurrent}

1

~ outer ~ day 1

5

~ inner ~ day 2

43

~ secret ~ day 3

89

{outercurrent}

119

bibliography

123

Manatee/Humanity

{ undercurrent }

This poem takes its initial inspiration from a particular initiation/teaching—or *wang* (literally "empowerment")—in the Tibetan Buddhist tradition, with links to a pre-Vedic shamanic ritual, and from an encounter and meditation on the mysterious manatee, the endangered mammal of coastal waters, and the grey wolf, residing particularly in the western United States. The poem emerged as a kind of urgent discourse. The Buddhist initiation is named *Kalachakra*, or "Wheel of Time," and has been granted in recent years with accelerated frequency in both Asia and the West. The view is that such an initiation confers power and permission to enter into specific meditative practices of empathy for achieving "enlightenment" (clear seeing) in order to benefit others (including the plant and animal realms) as quickly as possible! It also investigates the nature of time and change.

Tantra refers to a stream of continuity, or thread. This ongoing stream is our own mind, which in the Buddhist view continues through lifetimes. At it subtlest level the mind is known as "primordial pure light" and is free of the oscillations of conceptual thought or disturbing emotions. It presumably underlies every moment of experience, awake or asleep—like a radio that is always on, playing ceaselessly even between bands, or while turning/tuning into another frequency. Our mind is the basis for our experiences of death; our experiences in the *bardo*, which is the state between rebirths; and our conception of a new life. Neither the possible static nor the volume or the particular station affects the fact that the radio is *on*.

From a parallel perspective, neither intensity of our experience nor the dramas of our discursive thoughts and moods affect the "clear light mind" that is also on. Each stream of continuity is individual as well. All radios are not the same, although their receivers work the same way. In this view, there is no such thing as a universal mind in which our minds all participate, but rather myriad unique individual pathways, innumerable possibilities. One of Jack Spicer's metaphors for the poet is the radio; the poet is always on. And what is the mind of manatee? was a question for this poem. There seemed something wonderfully cognizant and primordial and *on* in the manatee spirit, albeit at a less speedy frequency. I remember William Burroughs sensing (maybe riffing on something Jack Kerouac had said) that so many animals seem to be in *samādhi*. He thought this of his cats, and he said often that he would prefer the company of lemurs to that of humans.

Tantric practice uses the imagination for visualization, in order to identify and invoke certain energies with one's own mind and body. It is essentially a practice of empathy. The rainbow-colored Kalachakra deity has four faces and twenty-four arms, and a consort with four faces and eight arms. The more arms, the more power of action and efficacy. Traditionally one visualizes one's self as the deity during the initiation to conjure greater compassion and then dissolves the image at the close of it.

The mandala or map created for such an event is of a symbolic universe. It describes a palace and surrounding grounds where the Buddha figure dwells, which the initiate enters imaginatively. Like the parts of our body, each architectural feature corresponds or refers to a realization that we need to maintain activity in our minds. A mandala may be a three-dimensional structure, and a mandala made of colored powders or sand is a blueprint of that structure.

The initiation with preliminary preparations takes three days.

I received this initiation with several hundred people on two separate occasions some years ago. The guides were renowned meditation teachers in the Tibetan Buddhist lineage. I was struck by the highly ritualized and lush nature of the three-day "doings" the first time, not at all sure I was comprehending the slightest essence of the Kalachakra's profundities. And I certainly felt inept and clumsy trying to follow all of the instructions and complicated visualizations. Entering the initiation we were given two pieces of kusha grass—one short, one long. We were told to place the short one under the pillow and the long one under the mattress where we sleep, and to observe our dreams. My particular dream was of the Armageddon variety: somewhat terrifying, with dismembered and eviscerated human and animal corpses lying about as in a classic war zone or brutal abattoir. I remember hiding in an alleyway with forbidden "sacred poetry" books that were also under siege and were to be quickly memorized. Yet there was an alternative to this dark vision—one of escape and of a community of others in the same predicament. We were being helped by aquatic creatures. I remembered the story of my Huguenot ancestor escaping persecution across the Atlantic with the family bible hidden in a loaf of bread. The kusha grass is supposed to purify inauspicious dreams.

I thought as I awoke that the dream was the very reality that the Kalachakra initiation was meant to cope with; that this advanced ceremony was being made available to many, including those not necessarily Buddhist, as a way to work against the insanity of the increasingly dark and corpse-strewn *Kali Yuga*, or "Dark Age"—an age where war and suffering and inhumanity seem pathologically endless. The view, as I understood it to be, was to get free of the samsaric wheel, at least comprehend how time, space, matter, and especially mind or consciousness work. I remember thinking during the large gathering that although my first Kalachakra initiation seemed like theater (at one point the initiates were wearing blindfolds) or pure fantasy, we were putting our bodies inside this creation—this vivid spectacle—toward some elevated purpose. I thought of Antonin Artaud's sense of the theater being the place or "state" where one comprehends the human anatomy and that with the human anatomy one can "heal and direct life."

As such, the text of the Kalachakra initiation moves through numerous descriptions of both macrocosm and microcosm, examining external and internal and "other" (outer, inner, secret) details of the environment, the body, the stars, and even the finest increments of atoms and molecules. Time in Buddhism is primarily a measure of *change*. In fact, time is understood to have no beginning or end, but only the reality of change. "What does not change is the will to change" is the oft-celebrated line from Heraclitus. Universe, civilizations, and life-forms rise and fall. Liberation from time means liberation from confusion, from an erroneous view of how things actually occur.

The poem is an investigation into and an improvisation upon some of the ideas and concerns of the Kalachakra layered with a vow of *take all the animals with you in your life, your poetry.* This is not systematically or linearly presented, however, and the poem eschews most of the points of minutiae that a visualization of the atoms of the body and the universe entails. How many breaths we take in one day or the complex systems of astrology used for making predictions seemed hard to capture systematically. Or the descriptions of the precepts concerning the twenty-five modes of "tamed behavior."

What is so astonishing in the obsessive ritual descriptions, however, is the vision of a "person," how complicated that is, and then what it takes to unravel and "purify" the conditions of the mind of that "person" and set it on another more beneficent path. What is sentience? What is consciousness? What is humanity? What is empathy?

What primarily interested me, however, is the intersection of the wisdom, descriptions, and presumed efficacies of the Kalachakra with modern neuroscience concerning the nature of mind and of consciousness in the brain theater. I became driven by the notion of "mirror neurons" as a way to understand leaps of sympathy and inspiration in the human condition. Some of the practices of Tibetan Buddhism—such as visualizing icons, seed syllables, deities, and so on—are meant to imitate and lead to states of consciousness, awareness, and empathy that counter the normal tendency to disconnect from "other" and maintain the territory of personal ego.

Finally, invoking the gnosis of the natural environment and its denizens as recommended in the mandala of the Kalachakra initiation, I summon life-forms that seem particularly threatened. The poem's litanies of the manatee and lemur and the wolf-dream are meant as lyrical interludes—modal structures—of both plea and restitution, and they stand in for all endangered species. The day a few years ago in Miami when I spent several hours in the presence of a wounded manatee in a local "sea park" was key to this project. I vowed to "include manatee." I believe it was a "she" who had weathered human harm and neglect. She seemed an ancient soul, and contemplative in her demeanor—huge, Buddha-like—and I fancied that I received transmission from her example, which was as a witness to cruel captivity.

The Buddhist view is that all life-forms are interrelated through their evolutionary history and that animal and human minds are both participants in reality. We share the planet with many non-human temporalities. Minds exist at the quantum level, below the level of atoms and subatomic particles. As is said: Minds never come from nothing or go to nothing.

I visualized the manatee's realm in the shallow pool as a shrine. I perceived her less as a victim and more as a poetic deity. And I felt she had the greater sympathy for me. The manatee ostensibly has no *use* in the current world. It's odd how creatures pacifistic, transcendent even, go extinct as human realms of cruelty, plunder, and war grind on.

~ outer ~

day 1

~~~~~~

Study density of
maxed-out earth-planet-universe
Study our captivity, o humanoids
Zoom in on the bald cypress
or *Haliaeetus leucocephalus* (bald eagle stalker)
Consider our exile, depravity in a strange laboratory
Is it a cosmic contest
who is the most backward barbaric bellicose greedy
psychopath?
Or who scries the future with greatest unsurpassable wisdom
Scries delicate muscle of land & sea, predicts the trouble spots
of flood tempest famine the curling hurricane with its
black & blue eye of all storms
devastating deleterious cyclone
no hiding place down here!
Do I have to choose/compete
Will there e'er be a better time, o humanoids
for endangered inhabitants, critically harmed ones
Animalized spirits plead you out of
inexhaustible (*till they drop*) eco-dream & delirium
enough, *enough! Kefaya!*
They talk & the dead talk too
Tell of mythic wonder & fragility
in zodiacal light
Tell how the meaning of *sentience* as in
the ability to experience suffering

makes us all kin
Tell of lovemaking under lindens
weedy glee—remember?
Tell of magical beasts & weeping trees
cross wounded galaxies like meteors or as crystalline deities
all particles reflected exposed rehearsed
by a magnanimous sunny disposition to survive—
devour, destroy yet *survive*! or . . . ?
You who keep all this going in language,
O language brains
who speaks for the wild universe?
Who goes down to the count
O mute promise of bunnies overpopulating the sod
Utopic possibility, burning brain
O cutthroat language!
I am truly on fire
Dear definitive new Darwin, where are you?
Or rather *where is she?*
Hiding in the mandible scriptorium,
the slime mold lab?
Standing on a rapidly melting habitat
with the polar bear?
Tell us what we are
Did we do it all wrong for survival mode
Did we screw up?
Can I make it up, try, overcome, desist, resist, blossom again
Buck the system in cyborgian mode
with synthetic flashback mechanism
with military precision techniques
with projectile costume of vamp & dare
& stiletto
the better to enhance you by . . . or
breathe & wait for next hallucination?
Give me orders I'm soldiering fortune
Is this not a torture trap version of unfittest world?
With trepanned head my thinking
so weird & complicated now

by end-of-world scenarios,
end-of-history dramas where I
can't think straight
mind queered in every direction
genre, gender, zonal, racial as the definitions
bleed together—freaked, torqued
damaged—with this wounded head I embrace the poem
I said I would move from A to Z
Travel all the years with you, millennial
I said I would be all constituents
& ride many continents
I said I would intone my litany of curiosity
I would dance with the language & dialects of bees
I would be mummified to speak the Egyptian way
out of cranial stuffing, messing with circadian rhythms
Let's agree on the symbols dear partners in sound
To get across this passion & heat
I would keep the syntax of sorrow in April
Grief on every side can't withstand itself
But it must be said in April it must begin in April
Sweet April with frogs & crickets,
& precession of equinoxes, o activator ram!
But do with experiment of empathy all I must
identify in empathy — You too
& the light of a hundred thousand buddhas
guide us
A head just barely "on"
held by a gorgeous scarf
of rainbows & galaxies
& the tiniest stars & fireballs
& zenithal projections
& tales of the Zheng He expeditions
when China tried to tie up the world
with trade she would be an example
of reach of time & space
I am no zoologist
but field poet

with a zygomatic arch
with tender love of the manatee
What century are we in that threatens manatee
Please come home to me in this one
my darling, my love, my friend, companion
who sings of all this too
& you, manatee, you join in this *Convivio*
Meet me in Broca's area
Wernicke's area, by the edge
of supramarginal gyrus, angular gyrus,
at the primary auditory cortex
I will be waiting
O zephyr o zephyr lily
all the lilies come too
& radiant colors of zither I play
to aid the task of liturgical assignment
arrive
Study humanity's expansion
humanity's destruction
neuroscience's lilt & tilt
& get back to me,
Dear You in our conversation
unspecified "you" or you I'm talking to
Zero growth
Young blood
Youngster theory
Youthful offender
You you you
Yucatec or yucca moth
You who throb I'm coming nearer you
It's bright jumpy Tuesday
We're hoping some kind of weather arrives
might resemble spring
Red wings keep up quite a racket
Buds deciding whether it's safe yet or not
hold back?
Keep alert here

If I could see you, masticating humanoid,
as Siberian tiger, grey wolf
as hairy-eared dwarf lemur
as cheetah as blue whale
If I could but see you morph as snow leopard
Uncia uncia or *Panthera*?
Track you from Afghanistan to Lake Baikal & eastern Tibet
with your ringed ash-brown spots
& elegant rosettes of black
stalking your prey . . .

what if

~~~~~~

& why did my brain incubate all those long years

& why was it not using its genius to make fire

& why not art the making of which would stir neurons further
& touching the texture of stone, shaping hand to stone
putting marks upon it further

& why not   why

to further beauty in the making of art

& why in sound too, not making music all those long years

sounds imitate what must have been the call of birds or of the body

in internal *hum* & *chatter* & *growl, chit* & *whooo wooo wooo*

parts of the body convening together as alluvial, as sound together "alluvial" "alluvial"

in strange harmony or discord too or in hunger need desire

fighting in all the discords of desire & wooing too

signal distress signal delight signal the stark moon you see & eclipsing of it

signal distress signal delight signal redress mistress redress & holy moon

& cry when the moon disappears, returns & celebrate by dancing

why did not my brain dance all those long years

would this not be in the frame of that incubation

its calibration toward gender toward yearning toward other particulars of size & gaze & color

how many thousands of years & between all & what is human thousands of possibilities constituting reconstituting

thousands upon thousands

& why did my brain incubate all those long years not using its genius to make fire

cry for water with a parched sound & why, how could it with slow memory without knowledge of itself now growing moving slowly know itself—why

this the ur-world keep silent within long, vast, still silence then grow into sound & sounding

no need for anything to grow from my fingers grow from moist womb yet

but what would grow naturally of sound & sounding what will to fight &
grow

tongue to speak & know that love is reciprocated

& when injured to cry out in panic surely

& when in making of love to cry out also surely in panic in pleasure

& in coming to birth, cry

speak about coming to birth pleasure making love & panic, cry

& you speak about eyes that lock together, a pair of heads together

not occlude but of dimmer now coming-to-light in wit mutual

or when the consciousness can look at itself know its wit & fractured rhythm

& when in making of love to cry out surely & fiercely, cry cry

in coming to birth to cry out decidedly a long cry

of mother & in death too, a discordant wail

in minor keys & all the ululation

why did the brain incubate all those years

why not using its incalculable genius to make fire

my what size you are my hominid & of intellect, not strewn about

why are you at the root of my word *lanthanien*—to escape notice

why do you explore the periphery of *latere*—to lie hidden

inside a universe with a hidden dimension

one tries curling up inside of

what if & why

& heard "why not" explore realms of

"where we meet"

~~~~~~

Oldowan stone of irregular edge cuts another stone crudely
stone of irregular edge cuts broodingly
old woman old woman hold the blunt instrument to soothe thee
or Acheulean more gracile hammer flakes off stone rue thee
& vocal in the cry of hunt "kill!"—what? kill thee?

primate surprise

"chieftain"
so named by Linnaeus

survival mechanism

self-recognizing

prosimian   mirror
neuron

she stood up
shrill, hurried conversation
expressing sorrow
"o snared swan"

once in the mirror
backlit by sun
beauty "me," a snared swan

I excite you,
gesticulate
modern heterosexist
presumption
not
in place by
candlelight

you are
beauty "you"
moving up the ladder
of this spine

& I a fragmented "me"
(do mirrors have eyes?)
with bestial affection for you
of kin but no matter

of purpose shatter
would a shepherdess be
in eclogue splendor
if she could but be
those cranial valleys & stars

both by kin of this action
left hand lifts   kind palm open
hands free for greater locomotion
out on open savannah
slope of
beckoning
now swing   turn   grab
a kindred object
how you feel
attraction
hold, offer
a mandible heart

cross-dressed body
puts on syncretic pelt
& moves as in
plucky mating dance

stabs at promise
tongue's word
stand up looking eye to eye

my grip around your legs

{footprints at Laetoli:
three australopithecines
crossed a carpet of fresh volcanic ash
walking much as we do
in two-legged gait}

hip & leg gone much the way
toward human form in place
of what in apes suits them for swinging
through trees, scamper on all fours
across a line that leads to man

clutch a mind
held tight together
in proprio-perception
of you mordant, sweet maybe
the grand occasion
laboratory for kindred study
all my mammalian characters
hybrids

not mirror stigmata

moving under sine waves together

his name
is her heart again, sign off

& the distraction of
his/her/one's monkey mind!
makes me wild
again
donkey telephone
donkey strife
the saint in me
abandoned
light rails of
imperceptible emotion
supersonic lifestyle
jet off again
carbon hoofprint

catch me
watch you
catch me
watching

humanity performs the same action
wherever "it" travels
tiled roof . . . mud wall . . .
thatch hut war zone tent shanty
gradients of . . . "to cross a bridge"?
to cross a Bering Strait?
all traits at play . . .

(humanity plays at dying plays at vanity
all 'ings & 'itys & 'thys)

dear humanity:
please do not end this time in slaughter
you've traveled so long & hard . . .

you too   or me   empathetically
I struggle   inside you   my biped
follow/fallow
talk/squawk
primp/preen
this is furnace/*light up*
this is auto-da-fé/*light more fiercely burns*
this is torture/*recoil, wince, scream*
this is love in the labyrinth/*uncertainty*
this is murder in the labyrinth/*atrocity*

chimp see chimp do a shell game
find artifice? chimp "know thyself"
in mirror-recognition

mother-to-son:
this is the way we operate down here
in virtual humanity

monkey-under-the-scalpel   test monkey
task tedium monkey
pity for you the long afternoons examining the validity of a hypothesis

unplug monkey from the neuroscience machines!

such a cell might recognize a gesture, wave
in jittery
feeling-tone
love or horror
such simple test, glass on a table
light through her hair
someone held against will
silence initiates the first experiment
raise a hand in jest & build your neural cargo cult
& fly out of here, stiff pantomime

impersonate an incursion in the cage
(manatee brain floats in jar on the scientist's desk)

pick up the tablet
pick up the stone
hold the mirror to the beating heart
now ripped from its cavity
turn it over
do not eat this thing

does the bird understand its oviparous offspring?
do not eat this thing

& would that thought be motor or sensory?
& would that thought occur to you anyway
worrying your accounts & time sheets
below bedsheets worrying your
muscles & tendons, your sexual prowess

I ask the drawn-out day all jittery again, of you . . .
to set you humanly free

please water the mirror of this thought . . .

jump to make this case

direct attention/choose experience . . .
ribald   random

& important changes
in the throat structure allowed the sounds
uttered by *homo erectus* to approximate human speech

glance that diverts
& darts

& recent pictograms
from Tigris & Euphrates
were the origin of this poem
5,000 years ago
& you are suddenly
outside
what you thought
you saw, you a gazing-one,
watcher, seer
maiden of the laboratory
with shock wires
probes   calibrating tools

measuring

what you are not,
what was just in there, not lost but
what went wobbly, water-tailed, winged
where language held your hand in
too-freighted kinship

attention boosts measure
the salience of its target
talks
& gets booted off a spectrum

salience of neural representation so
related to the activity of cells serving it
that you jolt awake

Eureka! I got it, my *mind*!
a net of jewels . . .

diamonds of alliance or dalliance
skin grows back invisibly
in the dark forest
to cover this treasure trove

attention increases the discharge rate
of neurons coding for a target
as you get their attention
& walk in the room

all eyes on you, target-trove

as if imprinted on chest
arrows come at you

from the dominant tribe
that sunk many animals

a living legend
in her leopard dress

seeing is always "seeing as . . ."

as "art educates perception"

they were called "thunderstones," a kind of folk etiology
they were thought to be lightning strikes or elf-shot missiles

hominids of the lower Paleolithic on whom the leopard preyed knew this

& thinking: was what you came from
how you behaved?
in view of the welcoming gallery
locked in a museum now, of value
only atavistic?
the manikins in their distress positions
tableaux of resistance & survival
women at cook-pots

men hunkered down over core tools
pebble choppers, bifaces

lithic reduction all in concert in a battle-ax culture

quartz, quartzite, basalt, obsidian,
later flint & chert
to advance consciousness, vocal cords even more evolving &
she bends to caress the puppet-child in the display case
a wild wolf-dog at her feet, "hush now"

I tell you *any rock that holds an edge will do*

to activate a narcoleptic brain
&
that was my first sentence

any rock that holds an edge will do

I mumbled this in sweet ur-time
when I was naked
when I had desire
that we might survive
& get the human exploitation
off the sharp edge

(animals butchered by tools included waterbuck, hartebeest,
springbok, zebra)

& I thought of reflexivity

to suckle
& had I a chance?

had I a chance in this form?

Kamchatka Expedition 1741–1742

Captain Vitus Bering & two ships—
St. Peter & *St. Paul*—were
on their way home to Kamchatka
following an expedition
to map the coast of Alaska
for Tsar Peter I the Great of Russia
    & spotted the creatures

& hidden behind them, their ancestors

ancestors of Steller's sea cow:

Dusisiren dewana & *Dusisiren jordani* were once widely distributed

around the Pacific Rim from Baja to Japan
where
Hydrodamalis thrived until the coming of humans
in the Pleistocene

Dusisiren jordani was common in the shallow coastal waters of the late Miocene,
California 10–12 million years ago

order of *Sirenia* near African in the early Eocene 45–50 million years ago

the term comes from Haitian word *manati* for "breast"

breasts like women's that suckled their young

Carib *manattoui*

Manattouf
maybe Mandingo origin
given by Spanish colonists
Latinized as *manatus*
infrasound produced in larynx
Ojibwa: *manitoo*

turned with its hands

handlike form & handlike use of the fore flippers
& I thought *manteuesthai*, to prophesy
had I a chance in this form?
Humanity *manifestus* (caught in the act . . . of . . .)

& in the dream he/she is fast upon me
& in the dream I suckle him/her/one as close as domestication allows
& in this dream had I a chance

~~~~~~

                                        everything is some thing else
        to eat   good means *good to eat*   all the pronouns
~~~~~~

They had decided to walk to the ferryboat now

the map of the lakes lay on the table

she picked up the book close by, setting the map aside
& as she approached it now more closely, now looking at it, she was happy to see—
& she did this quickly—lifted as she was by the title, the photographs within—

walls   a superimposition

of a she-wolf's face

it was a book by a friend
        the name of a friend clearly on it whose writing she admired
it was lateral writing, a kind of meditation, on the detritus & refuse & vast sweep of
time's ravage upon many great cities

diasporas of

        visible & invisible migrations

subsequent incursions

that make their curious
        desperate mark on the faces of cities

    a photo of the friend stares out squarely
defiant she might say knowing him but perhaps not
        more certain of the credibility of line & mark & point
of puncture & fury.   he was one to walk a lot
& comment upon the certainty of seething & disploding peoples
        of people pulled to the maelstrom of survival—
                    of them
pushing & pulling tug at this . . . what you say? string?   a life
line
        & backstreets, places by water   melancholy survival-deals

that dealt a raw hand

  he had traveled to the undersides of them
    indefatigably
                    &
lived in the interstices
        watching those cities below her imagination
what he had seen

what he had seen below the imagination
he had seen odd delineations of fear & seething & disploding
    juxtaposed with mad delight of martyrdom
    how implodes everywhere

the ethos "by any necessary means"
    he meant they were crowded like rats
or like the circumpolar "head" people living under the sea—
ghosts consisting only of a head
ghosts waiting to be buried off the killing fields of Srebrenica

darker districts outside Paris where the trouble they complain of arrives from

she thought of semaphores
he was trying to tell her something with his signals
with his codes & flags & where they might measure "distress"
could measure "help them now"
signal "distress, distress"

it was words, words only now, here, the ferry close by
within walking from their temporary shelter
he was of the words-only school,
then turning words to movies
those moving-pictures impersonating shadows
a moving-pictures school
& movies
movies-only

for you could tell in light, he would say, words
    & he liked them dark, transgressive even

& what are you wishing on I mean "working," "working" on? he asked

"chewing on the mammal"

it was like an hallucination
first the objects strewn about where they had arrived from
a book, a map, quadrants discarded now
a sense of the shelter & the departing from it
map cast aside, they would try their luck

his caverns of cities weight of them in him
in her mind now
they had sat with their lunch on another ferry
Lago di Como   animal bereft
lithic underpinnings
& the writing they both did took you to those other places
waves on the Bosporus: Istanbul
                    or Cambodia

they both wrote as if in the grip of a fever
(—have you ever had the terrible dengue?)
  because of urgency,
survival

to describe the known world of any reach or stretch of imagination

        the relative world of death & change

with the machinations of capitalism grinding away, charged & mysterious
        brute force & decimation
deracination
was her time irreversible?
how many objects put to the test
  taken apart
deconstruct them into their essential nature:
  compassion!

name outliving the person who carries it as with a book
name   identity   "person"
  & have you heard
  he asked

of the continent of detritus—100,000 pounds of petroleum plastic?
  twice the size of your continent (he was not American-born)
      churning in a vortex
  & the water animals under the intense burden of naming

how else we know them
by their sound
by their cry?
  struggling in the serpent coils of plastic, marred
scarred

& she wondered
what animals must be sacrificed to the colonization of time?
to the colonization of cities

colonization of oceans?
of planets

when science doesn't find something
she mused two possibilities toward him in her philosophy
        the not finding of something that doesn't exist & the case of
even though something exists it can't be found
    do you know what I say of this

not exactly the purpose

past & future lives who is to say they don't exist even if you cannot find them?

& he:
there is a world, that is enough, start here & purify

the external environment, start here. I began in cities

if there are sides, there is a center

the Milky Way has a center around which it revolves

one billion light-years across . . .

she: earth?

you mean this book might be my center she hoped she prophesied?

(eager)

like to go there he said, with you he said
& picking up her thought
        like wind's cognition . . . said:

again, what is unmistaken?

& she: *I know him, I know my friend*
by looking at him in my mirror of him . . .

& we rode then many miles
when riding was a way of thinking, investigating
places . . . people . . . animals . . .
some miles of them, "tribes & all"
& in sympathy, being magic-ones, poet-ones
because we could ride out in another century
& bring the past along

wondering

what

  animal

  traps

the

"what of"?

what of animal cages?

        & troops (we saw them embarking in the distance)

what traps the troops?

                & torture (unseen) but you see it in the mind

most impossible a subject which becomes a (trapped) factor of life

~~~~~~

mere trappings, razor wires

meant

"torching"
  meant "lynching"

& summoning animals to the hunt
dressed in their skins
with gestures & sounds from the vibrating larynx
sing of becoming them

being them
eating them

animals

    of

  troubled

descent

or
    "sewing
  the
      starflower shirts
by which the birds would
    be
brought back

to human

shape"

& on the slow ferry ride (they'd now boarded) she continued further her mantic dreams
how they'd come to her as Voices

"a previous universe might disappear & there is an eon of emptiness—
or eons of disintegration, followed by eons of emptiness & during the
twenty intermediate eons of emptiness there are particles of space
& that's where you come in"

she started in her cave-mind
a particle of space
how "come in"?

more Voices

"during the eons of arising the basis for the arising of space, wind, fire,
earth, water are the particles of space"

she started thinking about arising
she observed her breath on the windowpane (they were inside the hull of the boat
now)

"within the cognitive source which is all phenomena arise forms that come
from mental storehouses, generating compassion—such as vows"

she thought about vows, might she take them toward him, toward humanity?

"those existing in actual situations such astronomical & microscopic dis-
tances between things, those that are totally imaginary—such as those
perceived in dreams—
& those from gaining control of the elements"

"as for those that come from storehouses—they cannot be seen by the eye,
they are like our atoms"

& he responded as if translating for her the notion of enlightenment: form has shape &
color—color implies wavelength frequency on a spectrometer . . .

first you have the "dissolution" sequence: earth, water, fire, wind, & space

then the "generation" sequence: wind, fire, water, & earth

externally what elements develop out of is space & what they dissolve into is space

& they noted the categories together
& in upon this "science," in upon the speaking of these things, he became more
forceful
as a geomancer might when listing impressions in a daybook

~~~~~~

1. Astronomy

heave "destiny"
(we are in the planetary observatory now
a new rock show on Mars
shiny silver pods in the sky
water & striation

how pass
wolf star you say
if only . . .
& are
 we
  star-crossed?
nuzzle me yr elliptic)

      took you to bed to make
you more intimate

compliance
tucked
into tamed speed

repeat the 100,000 million stars in the Milky Way
& how many inside us?
  one of every million orbited
by planets

10,000 million planetary
      systems
  this universe. Or
  "you do the math"

Milky Way = our axis our mountain? Meru,
        & the mons of Venus
lie atop
this love

~~~~~~

2. Geomancy

turn here sit down
        here's a corner, face the sun

Anne, listen it's geo=earth, plus
mantikos=of the soothsayer
come in here now inside the square with me . . .

walked in on
ceremonial festivities
flushed by
long
look
of
him. a tutor?
        whence have you come? what fourth corner?
on head
feel a tracery
of his
mocking

darting
eyes
       of blue veins transparent skin
echo of a sad folk song

coming round what mountain hey
coming round what mountain hey

the dragon currents of megalithic tombs, stone circles
where we stopped to pick up the intonation invoked in madmen

~~~~~~

3. Geography

quadrants different as a leaf & flower
a single plant

the room's keen sensuality
you say a vigor

stand at the crossroads
poor Spartan you are,
you say a geomancer instructed you?

  a rough truce these war years
spring over borders
on a frown
    among unconscious twigs & stones

parted lips

history as your field of inquiry, an open mouth

an illusion of what is so urgently required
our sanity?
secret journal, a boat
colored thread wrote this all down

peering over the side
I swam with the dolphins in the Banda Sea

~~~~~~

4. Eschatology

too scared
as a child of neural complexity
"be a child of illusion"

it feels like the end
in the ceremony

external environment & cosmos in which we live
manatee as some harbinger of the future as in *they will rise*

I went to Florida & spent some time in the warm water
they will rise indeed

scribe a wide arc
mute glow of dawn
the strange propulsion toward nuclear demise
which will alter all landscapes

~~~~~~

5. Space Particles

discrete measures, not a fabric as once thought
they move between eons, they say, discreetly

all universes are made of atomic particles

what is between the cycles of universes are empty eons

(galaxy contracts with all its metabolism into a black hole)

during empty eons the basic elements merely exist in potential form
waiting

a space particle is a trace of the grosser elemental particles of a universe that is no longer joined together

as the soothsayer's coin drops to the ground

the space particle of a particular universe during its empty eon is somewhat like a super-condensed kernel of its matter from which its next phase of expansion grows . . .

a black hole emits radiation as matter collapses into it & suggests a correlation between the life cycle of galaxies & of the universe

a parallel process that operates during each person's experience of
life & death

each person's intelligence & sympathy is not without characteristic solemnity & joy

~~~~~~

6. Outer Wheel

all of the above plus culture & resistance!

~~~~~~

7. Inner Wheel

~ *time cycles of breath taken by a person in a day:*
21,000 words or worlds

~ "other"

~ *other is what purifies*

~ or future is what purifies

~ *myth & story!*

~ but neurotransmitters!

~ yes, the fifth revolution: neuroscience

~ off the Wheel?

~ yes, a falcon gets off the wheel

~~~~~~

8. Phylogeny

how did ancestors come to be conscious in the evolutionary past?

the neuron, its ion channels & chemical transmitters date back to the origins
of multicellular life & then she walks in . . .

signaling "system, system," signaling "distress, distress" & she takes a
measure of signals, her life a neurological drama, "distress, distress"

~~~~~~

9. Ontogeny

brain of a 4-week embryo resembles that of a fish which swam 400 million
years ago
plasticity of synapses—thousands of billions of them
a waking state—

electricity tracks consciousness
& you want to know "brain"
the fleeting rhythms dance over the surface of,
then shift coalitions of neurons in the cortex
you want to know
you want to badly know & add

   "brain"

rhythms depend upon the activating system at the core of the
upper brain stem & the thalamus
chemicals it releases unlock the hemisphere to the information that
bombards us from the senses
   why are we conscious

why do we experience what happens in our brain why do we see colors,

  hear music,

   savor taste

why aren't these processes enacted in darkness in silence as they happen
without body without language, why?

a kind of lust happens

thinking . . .
afference
& in a part of us, anything might "go" "on"

                    why?

~~~~~~

10. Soteriology & Apotheosis

if you could imagine,

or visualize the entire Wheel of Time mandala in a drop
the size of a mustard seed at the tip on one's nose
& see the whites of the eyes of 722 deities
  all rooting for the enlightened you, the wide-awake you

if you could imagine an enemy, who would it be?

(visualize the whites of their eyes
don't shoot!)

would it not be the proverbial enemy within . . . *you?*

(why did my brain incubate all those long years . . .

plotting its domination & hunger for its own sweet entropy)

guarded in the night
        why would you not travel in this kind of visualization

  what not accomplish with 24 arms

as you shift the ecliptic . . . . .

*& thus ended the list of the categories & then began the
section of the binaries & as she heard & noted them another possibility arose of the
"mirror neuron passages" that were to be her investigation through the second day &
night*

*{the light was fading on the horizon
& they "parted together" at the dock
Singapore is it? where next we will meet?
        or India . . .
                Elephanta Isle . . . perhaps*

*another ride
    "times out of mind"}*

*& in her vision
she saw "command"*

tablets/windows/binaries

*she had seen this in imagination
the split of worlds, of voices
the poet's "howl" in the canis lupus brain
hidden categories within categories breathing together*

~ inner ~

day 2

{ *lentissimo* }

If you could imagine, said again,
imagine knowing
elf kin

the "imagine" be in a kind of animal in
knowing

or resumed of knowing

If you might swell to it, imagining, kind,

or heroic but knowing

need, in need be needed in knowing of
kind

if not that kind talking back in dream that

feels urgent & a bond, needed to be next
to them & what they know

scientists, pilots

Needed to be next to them, elders

she knows herself
she is counting coup
the sexual frenzy
sexual priority
she knows herself
she is counting coup
everyone a partner in the
dream
everyone a wolf in the dream

in the body
of
large
swimming
  animal

morph to empathy
she knows herself
counting sex coup

but to *know*

toward yourself

inside

or inside "the nature of time"
All the breaths in one day resumed,

not manifest by chopped-up existence

anapest

    Count what is gap between but

  never calculating,

   not a pest!
   take the measure

  your winged chariot

who can presume hero or heroine

over
  plural

heterodox

the max to go to

      locality place advantage service

which is kind in thought of no beginning
staid stead
or "person"

abandon knowing
you are not the gnosis of
that word counting

she is standing tall
stood up on a leg
she is standing tall
came together, upright
all the personalities in
person to stand up, stand up tall
she takes the worried look
off her face

she locks it up in a music
box
she folds it up—fragile skin—
   in the music box

tomorrow the thick skin she
wears—
     of fur made—will
show the day

"person" that could move, resuming
identity

show the day
shows the day

"person"

instead of,
& out of mind

instead of condition

   action

fraught, as conscious

 I would be hurried now I would not
crawl by but stand

  urgent, not tarry

"person" & of all

standing tall

  safe in metabolism

no end first not world not sun not
something that might go out

do no slaughter
do not presume . . .
do not presume to slaughter

gyri & sulci

mollifies

her heuristic sense

she lives for emotions
she lives for emotions

of person

her passion
is not an analytic mind

   & her brain-scape

or his

   shapes in the gray matter,
the white
     "thinking" resides you say in gray?

her passion is appearance &
real cloudy water & the red
maples reflected
cloudy water cloudy water
& red maples reflected

I am the doctor or I am the glee of all
your evolution

As person with smaller brain, body just
the right size

  or "moxy" to sound it in steep hills &
deep valleys

literally held, in throat

toward an object

If you could imagine, of anyone of being
kind then

time leaking

that it might be, resumed, the future

drop by drop

as stuff

her time—her regenerative
time—
abandoning her time

  in perpetuity

 Give over to a way to operate, navigate

  how you might do no slaughter

choose & be kind

Draws down a bath
could walk & place a cup down about
there for you

Then someone else, for them

covers you with a soft cloth

Could take something out & move other
utensils around &

draw a deity in the sand

She

crouched in the dirt now, terrified

her not thinking externality anymore,
says again, her self
  alights in externality placed in relative
cosmos you say

conditioned in a kind cartouche

haltingly because cosmos is free &
disintegrating

how could you ever contain the child

in any war-torn, all of them, land that is
no father

that is again again father's revenge

& suffering

the land suffers & mothers suffer

how

taking a seat again, every day's relational

will he have her
will he take her
will he hold her
will he have her
drop by drop
secrets of battle
drop by drop

she does no slaughter
childhood fear
fear of slaughter
fear of animal slaughter

make no blunder today of that
that's no way to blunder,
slaughter
daughter of mercy daughter of
light

will she have her
will she have her
will she take her drop by drop

increments

  Write something down to resume &
counter then

  all attack (small medium large)

on scapes & species

down under, you are one of them

born a fish you would naturally be in
water

how sensible

  that the environment agrees with your
rebirth

she only a tongue

  agree

  Attoseconds
of suffering

& an eternity (cycles of revenge)

dart, the "arrow of time"

brush up against microfilaments

      time
spans of decay then a golden age, say
again, once ever
absent

something to conjure

**eyes eyes everything has them
everything
eye of the animal everywhere
everywhere**

**dear Big Oil, get out of here
dear Big Oil, out of the
picture
I'm performing at you out,
out we're watching you, Big Oil,
out out**

**she is standing in
performance
standing tall on legs
performing
saying this about Big Oil,
out out
the musculature of voice
she is counting coup, time
increments
memory, lifetime, memory, a
lifeline
better that Big Oil be out**

& then resume

would see pretend to see, would pretend
then see

the other way around, pretending in
externality to

ever see them, Other, them, the other
way around

presumed in imagination   **she adrift**

in this try, if resumed, a practice to get
off the wheel

Try   **beams of light**

not absent in any absented degree,
sweat & puff

not tarry as sophisticating emotions tarry

day no doubt

decisive for

no doubt presumed that you take it, never
        immune   **she gestures, understands,
performs**

in urgency   **she performs all manner of
"speakings"**

to the aboriginal memory, how presume   **welcome to her brain
to doubt?   architecture
welcome to her evolution**

Astronomy   **she will stand in for female
sociality**

    How many light-years back or   **neocortex glowing**

forward

could you go

    flip the ecliptic

More planets than you think in

that big brain of yours

Shadowy

& would there be consciousness

lurking there?

One planet might hide another or

one's planet might hide another

Refer, again, to dawning of "it" of "me"
of "day" of "hour" of "self" or "planet"

square will be empty
corner stacked
stalked by intruders

placental mammal!
placental mammal!

& a vow in kindness show, come in

barbarian we welcome you
  Celt or Etruscan

resumed to happen in presumption

a

femme fatale holding, now resumed

she is grasping objects now
she can do it
she can grasp
study her locomotion

open grasslands
open grasslands

in diacritical markup

Space yes perceptively charged "the idea
of me"!

announces

she is all that is well

how old a planet might be, said again,
how long
talking back to it/herself

& taking back the empathy, in a stride

she the notable pronoun always of
itself heard longer than uncertainly

to change a world

defense against "it"

her trying

&

push against "it"

  try on

autonomous could agree, say again,
fictitious "me"

or taking time

in time illusory?

in dilation

**she is soothing with her
breathing
she is soothing she is soothing**

**she is soothing with her
breathing
fine-tuned control of breathing
that's what it comes to**

**extra nerves extra nerves
in the thoracic spine**

**she is oracular performing
& standing
standing on her spine**

**open water
open water
now swimming on her spine**

Arising from vowels one might imagine,
notice,
& resume duration

If you could imagine "soon"

whale & dolphin
whale & dolphin

soon, a vowel "oo" sound

I'd wait how for you to be, to have been
in universe again, arriving soon

Does "soon" stop in the brain?

back to the cave
back to the cave

is detention like memory &
imagination
locked in?

or detection, slightly presumptive,
more enduring

bison & aurochs
bison & aurochs

& circular locked out?

belief-stance
belief-stance

 I'd say so, presumptuously

I would in elevation hot your act up or
hit it
running

ochre pigment & flowers
ochre pigment & flowers
buried alongside the bodies
all the tribal friends

& exist separately, hot–like,
with vowels

quantisized into deeper
distinct chronons

duration
duration

one is now passed

past maze & tense

torpor is passed you can go on longer,
past the soldier's tent

all the tribal friends

psyops of the dark world
en-tro-py of another

she controls fire
she controls fire

  moving down of past,
  past dawns

to choose from

a Neanderthal dream

              & physical objects may move
toward
future metabolism

& slaughters

How many

        how many

brains to say "slaughters"

  & might you ever end

  the criminal slaughters?

end to slaughter
end to slaughter

Entropy listen, & again, wait

slow down in a place no one forgives

what is it to be human
her bigger brain her bigger
brain

then resume a serpentine flow

it's a song her bigger brain

as in "the membrane was coiled
like a shell, significant, serpent seen
in the ear"

she is counting coup counting
coup in a bigger brain

magnificient

& could be entoptic

implicated in presumption of cornea, on
lens, & within 100,000 neuron cells

As in the center, resumed
to be a lotus which is weightier than "time"
"stellate" "basket" "granule" "chandelier"
"manatee"

contracting again
draw breath, resume the mind/brain
to make this day breath

how "I know together with"

my "scio" my "cum"

& prosimian fictitious even

or lemur I know, infer my "scio"

I make love

  therefore I know

& can explain

    hot love & again, resume

together with

I know together with my hot love

oracular
actually grown beyond,
moved beyond occipital "bun"
projecting mid-face
globe-shaped rear of skull
moved beyond, gone beyond
gone

or the dreaming snakes that
take you to an awakening
site & bite you back into
life

how sweet language enables this,
say again,
ancient & fragile language
ennobles this
& in mirror-self-recognition,

lemurian who might in quality

resemble

  you?

In hotter tone

who will obviate torture who
  in a rod of deep "can do" can do this:
tell time

this if we love

who will stop torture

  were to love & that would be plenty

How old & what conditions
prey upon each other
terrible world

irreversible Kali Yuga

  where we eat each other up

  weep rage

If one then with
quartz-like radiance in the eye

were to gaze

**dire world, crossing the straits
now
dire world, crossing the straits
now
dire wolf-world crossing the
straits**

**taiga tundra deserts forest
mountains
mountains forest deserts
tundra**

& where "you" the keys in the lock

to fit

in high old shaman time where resuming **to fit**

is always the way back around to
start over, resume, resume

What view from nowhere is, to ask?

   Tune the thighbone for eschatological   **she is giving you a dark look in**
time   **this creation myth**
                                                          she is the first to
Generate heroic kind reality   **experience death**
with stimulation of the phantom world
around

its

women who have been ill-used

around its

                                                          stepping stone set in white
animal study which has philology   **sand**
                                                          stepping stones set in white
around its instruments   **sand**
                                                          remind her of the Milky Way

Alter one genome
& you are
in consciousness assumed

         or presume to say
this

a particular style
& color

Just get that way, animal, okay?

a cloth being
resumed as impinging upon space

  resolved to be empty, & wrung

or gap between a world system

how implicate manatee

replicate
duplicate I know together with a vision
any idea of "kind ones"
to live always with the "kind animal ones"

&, resumed, as clear as water or sky
which is mysterious
dark

Gazing at the situation in general as it
folded all around

laughter carried
on the autumn air
laughter carried
on the autumn air

  & coiled you up in its dark plan

in a measuring rod of "deep time" as
coiling & spiraling out

Uranium-tipped danger could sing the
  end of you, coiled

or slaughters would they be visible, sing
of them

  lest they be forgotten

she is stomping in the fierce
urgency of now
stomping in the fierce
urgency of Now

Can you not feel the noise, slaughtering

the hello of it

Hello you horrible slaughters

Perception of world around you is made a
full slaughter

she is the spectral shift
she is the spectral shift

reflecting sound, mortar round

moving away from the known
universe

echolocation

Not seen not felt nor acted upon in
salvage/savage/slaughter

gamma ray bursts gamma ray
bursts
she is standing performing

but said, go, go away, so oblivious

Ignorance: can't look now

in a galaxy
in a galaxy
7 billion light-years away
7 billion light-years away

If you could imagine, refracted, say again
colloquially

   a better time

under guises of ordinary solar day

But justice? justice?

Now rage about it now, rage about it
justice just as it is is not justice

Apprehension unfold implode

threshold of language saying, kindly I will
not kill & animals with senses we do not
possess at all?

Not kill them too?

Soon my neuron is deciding to fire or
not to fire

choice by what mechanism? corny
empathy

Not wholly passive recipient of external
action resumed to be acculturated

your dense neuron star

Again, then

resumed

she is standing in for all the
animals
she is counting coup

spurn or spawn

how many animals to make
love to
how many animals to love

on empathy

Get you on this wheel to get you off it

tear my tongue from my mouth
if you dare
I am standing in for all of
them

metabolism calibrated

random in thicket in image in eye

terabytes & gigabytes

would you scorn

could you

whatever stars went to their
graves have been
dead before Earth & Sun
were born

just

walk

away?

or measure the calibration

Trying it on, there has got to be more
than one universe in this fucking
precious dark pathological time

Expand a portfolio that already includes
submarines tanks heavy artillery weapons
like the howitzer

or do not do this ever again

How wise is that doing?

You will roast in hell

criminal is that,
roast in hell, a mindset

What wit that criminal in that is that?

my wolf pulling back his ears in suspicion

my Ice Age survivor of the late Pleistocene

my narrow-eyed lover

my wolf going up & down the path of the
Milky Way
known as Wolf Road

my extirpated wolf in these parts
roaming the ponderosa & mixed conifer
forest

in the dream I am holding my kusha
grass, my grass of "pristine awareness"

crossing the white sand to
walk upon the water's edge
brittle stalks of autumn grass
brittle stalks of autumn grass

she performs to measure the
way
performs to measure that
animal way

bent under her chest
close to the heart

& human brain
will you lift up to that?

bent under chest standing or
performing sounding

she says this counting all
the atoms in her day
all the breaths in a day

temporal lobe
temporal lobe

bursting brain
bursting brain

when did

   consciousness

come on the scene?

what is chasing you

every day what kind of courage
every day what courage

all breaths in a day

no need to hide

61

&in the dream it was wolves all the way down,
       wolf pack thrashing & gnawing at the corpses of other animals
cannibal haven
misunderstood
a small splash, a chill

an eye caught
trapped!
stare!
quick!
       shift!
metallic shimmer
  cloaks & hoods of the imposters
rent apart by wolves
 "I am a youth with golden cymbals dancing"
then one, turns
           to me as in blame
would you come to my rescue?

reliable humans? would you?
 notice animals dressed as humans now, imposter humans

      strewn out on the charnel ground, clothed
battered & trying to be animal again, scratch wolf-eyes off the facade of human

images of many ravage sites flash by
   as if there is atavistic memory
creation of a perceptual world of death & destruction
long evolutionary gestation of death & destruction

           we stopped to observe (my companion always with me now):

cougar, head snapped
entrails ripped out . . . & spread all around
those parts not eaten
cougar cubs eviscerated, killer instinct or survival

what can we learn from the predatory nature of other animals
to surround the bison
down the cattle

the other way around, you said
we came first
  so like them . . .

we in our sweet-smelling realm so like them—
pack of wolves

    & all breaths escape to exhale in the continued plight of
wolves, loyal in their pack abode, cunning
bright-eyed ones

    wolfskin!
      ride over me tonight

& manatee
you can't mix a human monster ever enough up to aid the manatee

surely our conscious plans have precursors in animal brains

construct	**construct**	
a	**a primate**	
world	**of**	
of	**objects**	
objects	**(nail**	
space	**tooth**	
& time	**& claw)**	**space & time**

start here. Now.

now represent your representations in the symbolic code of language:
"manatee/humanity"

& run your hand along a restless spine

~~~~~~

it=was=time=of=fossil=fuel=priorities=of=precious=business=time

~~~~~~

that's what they'll say about us centuries hence it was a busy get on with it
business time so better-get-on-with-it-time, they fucked us all over in their
greedy get-over-it time

~~~~~~

that's what they'll say about us: what were they thinking? stupid fuckers
it was commodification fun-hog time, time-modification time, got on
with time we killed time they fucked us over in our future time we'll
be surely more stressed in time that's what they'll be saying that's what
they'll say: they got on with it, saying about us, going nowhere but going
down & us all with them, what were they thinking in their selfish minds,
us, us

~~~~~~

that's what they'll say about us generations hence (how living then hence
without so many animals then?) they fucked the world over in their sweet
avaricious time frame that's what they'll say, about us, those stupid fuckers,
they let the animals die, they let the plants die, they killed the air, they
killed the water, they killed each other, they killed language

~~~~~~

humdrum Paleolithic where we would talk in sweet time notches well that's
over where the fuck did that ever evolve to?

~~~~~~

then along 20,000 years of "keeping" time once keeping it for all & moving it, time, forward, & it, the art, forward, & it, humanity, forward, & now they want to kill it really they killed it

~~~~~~

then along rim of Babylonian, rim of Egyptian, 5,000 years once, ago, such "progress" they kill all that too, stupid fuckers

~~~~~~

then but now my solar day my lunar month my solar year, my speed I inherited from them, what time is it now?

~~~~~~

   & we resumed our talk—after these excessive outbreaks—discussing the nature of calibration

how different times give the peculiarities & particulars of people & praxis & place & thought systems, & become their own "zones" in this

we spoke of lustrations & the architectures of spiritual places, of constructing mandalas with colored sands & the women who dance on the precipice of eclipses . . . performance & ritual under arches, pillars that delineate the way to move as a chorus might, open atriums, they are moving into the augur's space, the place of frequent animal sacrifice . . .

we're mere sidereal time—two passages of the mean sun time, he cautioned, & that is relative . . .

   both, both, he cautioned further, it's quite unconscionably relative

(that doesn't explain I protested the way we brutalize time)

you may want to consider how an anomalistic year is the interval between two successive passages of the earth through the perihelion

(& this might be the year the four-legged animals take fright & hide, I added)

Julian & Gregorian is your solar time, this is your basis, remind you again you need a
relative time frame. start here

& what of animals on desperate clocks of survival & flood, famine, ice caps
melting . . . what of them?

polar bears exhausted, swimming over a hundred miles to shelter

of course, go mad with it

but you might consider the notion of proleptic time, brought forward, how one might
use devices

        in manipulation of time trick time? perhaps

or the first Sunday after first full moon marking Muhammad's emigration to Medina
July 25, 622 CE
called thus: Anno Hegirae *put power there*

called calends *(that power from* calare—*"to call out"); calends! calends!*

& then people will die or mythologize for a control of time

as when the Antikythera Mechanism organized
the ancient Greek calendar in the cycle of the Olympiad

so we are in mid-poem with a new moon, calling us out he laughed
in the forced monopolies of expendable time

Roman, Celts, Babylonians, Hebrews, Copts, 284 BCE
Zoroastrians 389 BCE
Ethiopians 7 CE
will honor you here
poem in its own time, an uncommon era

remember when a barley loan could be measured out to the lender at the next year's
threshing floor?

& the Himba people in Ekamba, Namibia, say when the thunderstorms start & the leaves grow from the ground, that's how we know it's the new year & the word for year is "rain," look up it's raining now

& looking down you might recognize the El Segundo Blue Butterfly who lives precariously in the shadow of the Los Angeles International Airport 2009 CE

& consider the severe declines of Coast Hosackia in your peregrinations
& the Lotus formosissimus *that supported this life*
most evident now
& old ponds gradually undergo a process known as eutrophication
which leads to dry land, 2050 CE

& gaze down again: a beautiful yellow nimbus outlines this shimmering pale blue butterfly in its pale blue butterfly time

Lotus Blue Butterfly in its rare coastal bog habitat

the Delhi Sands Flower-Loving Fly enters here, your mid-poem-life,

this is a test of the emerging alert system to challenge your existential day

sing manatee, manatee (you'd better praise all you can he said) all the trembling day . . .

& passing before her captivity
                    reiterating a chant of manatee
I began

the manatee is found in shallow slow-moving rivers

the manatee moves in estuaries moves in saltwater bays

the manatee in moving moves gently

the manatee is to be found in canals & coastal areas

the manatee is a migratory animal

the manatee is gentle & slow-moving

the manatee moves in slow-moving rivers slowly

the manatee is completely herbivorous

the West Indian manatee has no natural enemies

the manatee has no natural enemies but unnatural man

the manatee is constantly threatened by man unnaturally

man with his boats & plastic & attitude

the manatee often drowns in canal locks of man

man who makes no concession to manatee

the manatee dies in flood control structures

man who makes no concession to manatee

nor cares of manatee life manatee fortune

the manatee dies in collision with watercraft

man who does not protect the manatee

what steward of the earth is this unnatural man

man who makes no concession to manatee

the manatee dies with the ingestion of fishhooks

man who unnaturally makes no concession

the manatee dies from litter & monofilament lines

man who is rank in attitude has no use for manatee

the manatee dies entrapped in crab trap lines

the manatee dies from loss of habitat claimed by man

the manatee is maimed by man, the manatee could be aided by man

man o aid the manatee man come to the manatee heart

a manatee calf is born every 2–5 years

a manatee gestates for a year in the manatee womb

8,400 miles of tidal waters could be for the manatee

11,000 miles of rivers & streams could be for the manatee

10,000 miles of canals would they all be for the manatee

the manatee has more gray matter in the brain than man

the manatee is perhaps thinking archivally deeper than man

ancient days of manatee so many thousands of years

manatee mind, what is the mind of manatee

the manatee has no natural enemies

the manatee is completely herbivorous

the metabolism of the manatee is slow, moves slowly

the manatee moves in estuaries, moves in saltwater bays

the manatee moves in slow-moving rivers the manatee is gentle

the manatee offspring nurses for up to two years

the manatee learns everything from the manatee mother

the manatee mothers & offspring sing to one another

the manatee have large ear bones

chirps whistles squeaks of the manatee

the manatee in moving slowly moves gently

oscillations of the manatee moving between the manatee ears

ears of the manatee mother & manatee offspring

manatee are our sirenians, & live in the house of the sirens

where are the human sanctuaries for the manatee

manatees mermaids sirens singing move slowing

the manatee mother & calf so bonded

female manatee bonded with her just one manatee offspring

{*"There have been times when they come up out of the water and the light has been such that they did look like the head of a person"—James Powell, biologist, Wildlife Trust, St. Petersburg, Florida*}

in the ritual they said cast your lot in here

in the ritual you were meant to be protector

you were meant to be a progenitor

you were meant to rise from waves

mother . . . mother . . . *om manatee hum*

~~~~~~

& standing in the nimbus of that genus of strange species

as if saying, *this is the mind of manatee*

Manatee reminded me ~

that multiple
 hydra–headed
     universes,
all fractals in
    chaos
including more cycles
  will emerge

 formation,

  stabilization,
                        disintegration,
emptiness . . .

72

make it work give it a shape let it come apart

                                        start over constantly

formation:
stabilization:
disintegration
emptiness

some of your friends will be there, waiting

   the winds of karma provide the impulse for a particular universe to evolve
that comes from the collective karma of the clear-light-strife-gone-mind of
other beings who remain present during empty magma eons in between
universal autumnal epochs . . .

& these karma-winds provide the impulse for a specific birth to occur . . .

& speaking further, she went on, Manatee, fresh from her initiation into the
mysteries of time:

If in the grammatical structure of language you may speak of
 "iris," "nostril," "dazzle," or "across the dew-laden clover speak"
   hear passion flutter,
look down,
& when looking,
listen for
the cry of the manatee

resilient rustling void within
or
if, & then because of, & when

the world becomes treacherous
listen again

it may be lucid
   if what is meant is immediate, transparent
dangerous

you have unmediated resolution

   or
   silence

you have perhaps a few happy vignettes
vigilant of aspects of
   if & when you admitted it, a life

a life in struggle

of everyone broken in heartbreak
& the animals
experience that too

heartbreak

so restrained
   in admitting it

unlike humans crying all over town

& what kind of anchor, then, is time?

if in the grammar of sound it's always revolving around
  "what is the time of manatee?" or
"what sound caught in waves in manatee-larynx?"

a distinction between past

present

  future

then what is in relation here?

  Is how time strides

concentrically

  & inside time, an example of trance,

of samadhi?

we are in a kind of trance, said Manatee

that seems to occur outside time

then
  trace, belief, form,
abscond,

    & you become the witness of your impermanence
  & again

    you evolve around a distinction of past present future

how you will sound, distant wail through layers of time

& simultaneously

that which has no name sounds

then a lilt

  music of the sphericals

  flux refers to motion

   or an uncertainty principle

   or indeterminacy

how to merge quantum mechanics with general relativity

  you have your time organ in the brain

fret, grieve, worry, expect,
& experience nostalgia

mind never turns off nostalgia for a full moon April 15

~~~~~~

each stream of continuity being individual

& if it were not certainly like that, assuredly,
like stable that thing like that, just as it wasn't
in being a kind of contaminated pleasure

if then you would wonder: stability

retrograde now to direct your attention

& if the mind you could say, like the radio
is always *on*

whether or not it receives or is in gap or
frequency down, it is *on*

on relative reclaimed space

  or *on* absolutely
   on & *on* or *on* of certainty

on the lid of certainty

    or *on* the inner lid as it is putting a lid *on* uncertainty

its inner workings, mechanisms etcetera

in uncertainty as in a place to dwell certainly, asking another story
before the talk of barbarian hordes which are your own demons

what

are

the

implications

in a circular time frame

of such talk?

   is it loose?

is it cheap?

   is it responsible for a closed system?

is it misunderstood for its logical greed & despotism?

  who after all will control the energy?

who after all will be the master of the resources?

hyperconnectivity begets mimesis begets hyperempowerment

as we die out

& we resumed our conversation

   what had seemed ancient, a long time ago
to now be embarking
on a new life, a new style of poetry filled with yearning for the animal
but empty of animals remembered only in our naming of things after them
cars & trucks & teams & products that sap their mana

meeting after holocaust
         meeting after we had loved, been lovers
traveled to ends of some version of earth
      after we had been each other's own mothers

   he bowed to me, old friend
I shall never forget you
(said)
& confident of the future?

a difficult place? will you know me when you see me
know me as "what became a female body"?

I paused, amused
& he spoke to me thus out of his lemur-hood
as he called it, "a Burroughsian space," imitating the voice
of Captain Mission who looks after & cares for lemurs

& "if we are not extinct, what we have learned"
from them—& the many other ancient animals

the evolution of a female-driven social system in primates
& male deference is a social construct not a matter of size or strengths

lemur is derived from the Latin word meaning "spirits of the night"
lemurs are nocturnal with large reflective eyes & wailing cries
all lemurs (pygmy slow loris, crowned lemur, fat-tailed dwarf lemur, black
& white ruffed lemur, gray gentle lemur, ring-tailed lemur, aye-aye, slender
loris, slow loris, blue-eyed lemur, lesser bushbaby, collared lemur,
golden-crowned sifaka) have a "tapetum," a reflective layer over the retina
that causes their eyes to shine back light
lemurs evolved before anthropoids living during the Eocene epoch
55 million years ago
(the first monkey dates to 45 million years ago, the ape 35)
Madagascar broke from Africa 160 million years ago
did lemurs travel to Madagascar on clumps of vegetation?
lemurs are the closest living analogs to man's ancient primate ancestors
lemurs differ cognitively in the development of the associative areas of the brain
lemurs have scent glands on their feet that leave odors on the surfaces
  they cross
lemurs have a heightened sense of smell
lemurs are arboreal, spending much of their time in trees & bushes
lemurs have large bushy tails that wave in the air to communicate
their tails help them balance when they leap from tree to tree
lemurs have a good grip for hanging onto trees & branches

lemurs are well-groomed & use their teeth as a comb
some lemurs are hermetic, live alone, awake & active at night
others live in large stable groups & in fluid associations
lemurs show female dominance
lemur babies are carried in their mothers' mouths
lemurs are usually vegetarian, primarily eating leaves & fruit
as they move from flower to flower lemurs transfer pollen on their foreheads
all lemurs are found in Madagascar & the neighboring Comoros Islands
the forests of Madagascar are being destroyed at an alarming rate
50 different species of lemur are critically endangered
80% of their habitat has been destroyed
lemurs are hurt by new weapons & deforestation
lemurs are the most gravely endangered group of primates in the world

I was saying man's inhumanity to beasties
& then that thought swept across continents & consciousness
Where we all have been . . .
Reykjavík?
Denmark Strait, Nuuk. . . .
Notable for an arc. How conscious these places seem in an arc . . .
& thought of you, shape-shifting mammal
Love of you, cascades of it
Needing you warmer in armor
Garbled underwater, endangered

So this is your time. This is it.
A cage?

~~~~~~

quite a bit quieter in a cage
for I am sentient too . . .
"leaf consciousness"
said the leaf & won't you write this . . .
in atomic time? . . .
yes, my leaf . . .
in actual first poem time . . .

when you picked up the aboriginal ax . . .
(you'd made it, constructed it
how clever to be human)
proverbial ax it does sacrifice of animals . . .
& scratches in wet sand . . .
& building of shelter . . .
with chisel too . . .
hewn "characters" in the mind
arms & legs that are brisk strokes of language
dendritic, the shapes of our neurons . . .
your first language . . . gamma, insight . . .
anthropomorphic . . .
in pleasant jaguar language you are thinking . . .
in the tongue of the wapiti . . .
shape of leaf—like a *bodhi* flame . . .
paw of the dreamer . . .
who is stalker of prey . . .
aspirant, let's say . . .
for the kill . . .
blur of worlds as they tick by . . .
quizzical hairy appendages . . .
morphology all by itself . . .
between us, so many go down
does it ever end?
slaughter, does it?
& gone ravaging, gone back to the sea
without legs I a mermaiden be
before you
seaweed standing in my hair
come to my house of the sirens
morph this sea & land &
buck the boundaries
think always of you—tropical?
atavistic you wonder what
it takes to survive "person"
it's a different language below
a coastline & a manatee

limited by the human realm, heavy breathing?
inside what I could say
to stranger
gaze at manatee a good hour
comedic like you see on '50s TV reruns
tell me telepathically
what she knows about wounds
patience, endurance
familial love
communicates in
sonic system
signal "distress," "distress"
she knows "distress, distress"

the aquarium deserted now,
this is the song at dusk I write in the notebook:
strange skin
not quite seal
not quite dolphin
inchoate
texture like
something you forget
something you didn't even see
the first time
old shoe
sentient being with others in watery caves
lights off
with motive & mind up a ladder
mouth moving
quixotic mind
quick flick
who are me
who haunt me
please haunt me

summoned by the dream
the kusha grass instructs
you might say a kind of ceremony
gather up these nightmares
this in a public space
where many minds meet
& pass around the objects of this dream
a blindfold, a crystal, a card with a bodhisattva upon it
gather them up & making an offering
all the *bikkus* going down on their knees for this
in this world marked out by the augur
interstices between living & dead
an initiation on the nature of time
& of continuity in a dark time

mean world: humanity
dream world: manatee
secret world: *om mani padme manatee hum*
om mani humanity padme hum

the center of reference becomes movement in this ritual

~~~~~~

*they had boarded another boat (for the sake of riding, keep riding . . .) & her
companion had perceptibly changed
hard to describe now, morphing into
more of a voice (high-pitched what you might hear in the Bardo were you to listen)
because sounds had made a kind of syncretic power
between human & animal a force in the poem
all the sounds in the poem, all the breaths in one day*

delirium . . . dream . . . hallucination

she was inside completely inside

*I said I had hoped to see "it" all. Stopped the question. Beginning & end of humanity.
She'd seen it all, once. We walked wider. We joked about
weaponry on Mars. Someone would land a kind of nautilus. Tripping the wire there,
blue water. The whole house, as in an astrological one.
A foolscap, an appetite, an aperitif.
& if he/she were a furry animal, what kind of animal would he/she be? He/she was
an elder & I hadn't seen it all, incidentally.*

"zuzammen"
"entollen" hmmm.

what did these words mean?
Rooms & trolls.
we're worn, want to bet?
"Humanity is worn thin," he/she says & "it oughtn't be"
hominid species distributed through time . . .
homonyms through time . . .

honoris causa *in time*

It was the elder-poet-speaks-from-the-dead visitation, again
& what was the teaching?
That the dead speak & point their gaze on us
& that they sometimes speak in funny categories

~ & when you say "time" what do you mean

~ *an act of change*

~ & when you say "wheel" what is this

~ *something to ride off of*

~ come again?

~ *liberation*

~ from?

~ *from cycles of time*

enter like a child . . .

first, water
as if from a mother splashing as if after a child's birth

next, bind the hair-locks of the child when she is ready

three: pierce the child's ears for ornaments—for ribbons in the ears

four: you might be laughing & talking

five: the child enjoys five sense-objects

{shell for touch, smell a lily, taste this cube of fruit, a plastic horn sounds, a mirror reflects back at you}

six: naming "earth" "air" "fire" "water" & all the elements

seven: mantra, singing songs like the bubbling up of water

~ & then what?

~ *you are ready to enter*

~ what? ready to enter what?

~ *your own life*

& the participants studied the internal ceremonial code

analogy is "universe"/is "current had tangled"/is "esoteric venture"/
is "menagerie prescience"/is "teacup, a strange desire"/is "tabulation"/
is "restitution"/is "once a meaty quark"/is "any part her nutrient"/
is "recondite"/is *"porta principalis sinistra"*/is "phenomena meme text"/
is "verbal oral clarity"/is "metabolism"/is "calibrated spiral cortical
synchrony striatum integral melatonin"/is "my light of new millennium
don't abandon me here"/is "last chance estuary pineal brake"/is "nucleus
cycle pigment blood"/is "wavelength light pause"/

is circadian clock

circadian − circa + dies—as when I feel the pulse
late at night on MacDougal Street

looking to the animals there, Patti's cats, Ed's stoical & sartorial Jim
Chloe's Lita, a gentle wolf-dog
& the rats below

our pets resolve to abandon "revolution"

maintaining their oscillations frequencies rhythms in activity

leaf movements . . .

daily cycles of dark & light are your dictators who dictate when many
physiological processes that operate on 24-hour cycles will be most & least
active . . .

lie down with the wolf & sleep now . . .
your own neighborhood

~ secret ~

day 3

~~~~~~

Brain tracks fluctuations in light with the help of ganglion cells in the retina of the eye. A pigment in some of the cells—melanopsin—probably dictates light, leading the retinal ganglion cells to send information about brightness & duration to the suprachiasmatic nucleus of the brain. Then the suprachiasmatic nucleus dispatches the information to the parts of the brain & body that control circadian processes. Events lead the pineal gland to secrete melatonin. In response to daylight the suprachiasmatic nucleus emits signals that stop another brain region—the paraventricular nucleus—from producing a message that would ultimately result in melatonin's release. After dark, however, the suprachiasmatic releases the brake, allowing the paraventricular nucleus to relay a "secret melatonin" signal through neurons in the upper spine & the neck to the pineal gland . . .

long plane ride it helps transition from joy to sorrow or other way 'round . . .

interval timer

According to one model, the onset of an event lasting a familiar amount of time, the boiling of an egg, the yellow traffic light flicking on for four seconds, the cry of orgasm, the amount of time it takes after you ring the buzzer for a friend to respond & then the response mechanism unlocking the door you walk in, the time between the response that triggers the door & when it clicks open ~ I mean, the train leaves the station on time & will arrive exactly as predicted, we are in Kyoto now. Your "start button" is activated. The onset of this event whatever it may be in all the lives you have—past, present, future—announces we are in urgent Kyoto Accord Time now.

Time frame, expectation, hope or fear could result in a particular subset of cortical nerve cells firing at different rates & momentarily acting together prompting neurons of the *substantia nigra* to release a burst of the signaling chemical dopamine. Both signals then impinge on the spiny cells of the striatum which proceed to monitor the overall patterns of impulses coming in from the cortical cells after those neurons resume their various firing rates. Because the cortical cells act in synchrony at the start of the interval, the subsequent patterns occur in the same sequence every time & take a unique form when the end of the familiar interval is reached. At that point the striatum sends a "time's up" signal through other parts of the brain to the decision-making cortex . . .

The Defense Advanced Research Projects Agency is purportedly developing a neural implant to remotely control the movement of sharks. Sharks' unique sense would be exploited to provide data feedback in relation to enemy ships' movement & underwater explosives. To see & feel everything a shark does, understand the cortical plasticity of the brain. The sharks' natural ability to sense a weak magnetic & electric field is of particular interest to the military . . .

～～～～～～～～～～～～～～～～～～～～～～～～～～～～～～～～～～～～

shallow near-shore region

seaweeds live

swept forth or in limpid

swoon

a signal cannot reflect or elaborate upon

yet splendor there

& come to be there

mollusks

& naming them come to be there in them

swept down, come up to your evolution then in them

love for their not ambulatory-ness

sea snails & periwinkles

chitons & limpet

move as you do, inkling of vibration

& the common paua *Haliotis iris*

become metabolism

a wish driven

so deep it relishes the contrast

for human suck

motion humming

recursive

are minds possible without language?

luster not only for an archival eye

residual depth plea to The Wild

one day arrived at "chromosomal" time

or a water plant hypothesis called "nuclear"

(spy! spy! hunt! hunt!)

& you are once again a scare tactic

a smoke-out tactic

an Iran to break up a concept

that will never break in them as Other

while language reflects mind structures

strictures on ways to be in world

(are enemies aerial or terrestrial?)

not only data you crave

but darker pundit plans to know power

or else benthic animals (bottom-living ones) will go farther down

attach to rocks & stones & sediments

get food that way

filtering tiny planktonic animals or plants out of surrounding water

sponges   sea mosses   rock & mud oysters

or pipi & toheroa (*Amphidesma ventricosum*)

do this

what sound in your fleshly name

does this?

are you mere *matériel*

altricial? sexy?

half-cooked or cocked

made to be shattered by a bomb

are you fit in wit

& naming them thus come to be neural endgame

in gesture: three bows or blows wrought

in thought–pattern flight: three associations

accrete secret deplete

or larynx mouth & tongue

defensive

yet citizen are you?

speak out?

& that which destabilizes meaning my lover

is not you

& then there are the hidden colonies, multitudes of separate animals

all epifauna in this eerie survival game

neglect your sonar sexuality

neglect that cluster burst of sound

(listen for echo off a ship's hull that would deliver useful knowledge)

rethink the mouth of your disembodiment

ritual for the dead flint axes fire

Hedgehog depth charge launchers

antisubmarine missiles exist only

in a land of short sentences

lethal entrance

or keyboarding we live with

400 crude oil & toxic spills

Prudhoe oil fields

just thirty miles west of Arctic Refuge

adjusts intensity to the sound of refuge

deluge subterfuge death fugue

4,900 feet of deep hunting

you'd like would argue for the beaked whale

deep-water echinoids resting there

where she moves, antithesis

mitigated circumstance or resistance

oldest living seafloor animals ever saying something

excludes

her

or them?

"reckon 'round longer than

you'll ever be"

microbe time

"them consummate

mouth breathers!"

breeders

hover & suck up the air

directions of all possible space of

all possible global breathing

they are below

especially below.

& more below.

say: the coral reef is noisy today

it is a tendentious maze. if standing

a windy tundra always thinking about what the tundra used to be.
it was the sea.

if standing

& swimming?

say: all about microbes again in a mitochondrial tundra world

a Continental Divide: look

toward the Pacific & chant an open-air aria

or small song to coral, its inalienable

right to exist.

& nod to the East Coast

its shame. *where they run your life from* a dirge

& more below

my lover:

you are late before sunup

you'd better move upstream soon

~~~~~~

I'd asked did the universe exist before the beginning of time

an impulse of antithesis

* or is the bracket of matter*

phantom?

* transport & wandering*

the movie run back
metabolically speaking toward the Plio-Pleistocene

the atavistic wolf dream rubs into your DNA

* everyone a flake of time in the right brain hemisphere*

my archival time & language time & philosophical time & control & time all
synchronized

while on the left I am becoming more dexterous

& am continuing the mapping the territory for my poem's domain

& speaking now out of a Broca landscape

in a higher pitch

any rock that holds an edge will do

~~~~~~

We had stopped now, waiting for the edge of the drug to descend

                    you said come on in into the mandala of RNA
yours,
        mine

mapping your humanity to what purpose?
indeed, you said, as we approached the shore, you starting to shape-shift more
decidedly now

with some urgency
&

in philosophical time what is our purpose—
what is humanity's purpose in philosophical time?

habits that are in agitation in philosophical time
will wear out in philosophical time

fondness for struggle in philosophical time
won't wear out in philosophical time

to ramble did please us in philosophical time

but we were tempted to retaliate against philosophical time

shoulder on readiness in philosophical time

& soldier on
emissary for
the temperament in philosophical time
injustice?
everywhere
& in twilight, a philosophical time

empires were rising & falling in philosophical time

fossils
that might indicate
salvation
or
starvation appeared revelatory in philosophical time

chitons! braincase!
Afontova Gora on the Yenisei River!

we were happy to see them in philosophical time

the end of one civilization
could pop back in, more resilient
in philosophical time

a bitter touch of philosophical time

to touch it—dead history
how does it do itself, deadly,

to be that history
quite dead in philosophical time?
what did it ever learn
from itself or
from description of its own
charge & ineptitude
to strangle the translucent moment
when it becomes obscure in philosophical time?

empire upon empire in philosophical time?

what strange assimilation
of tasks & fortune
& willpower
got wound up in philosophical time

what is a mistake

what strange fossils that might
show
copies of
traits
& let the world come in, as petal, as small as petal

for one who once meant "strange" or
"in" for "mistake" or
"melancholy at the mouth"
like a movie actress known for this
"melancholy at mouth"
as a badge or downturn of fortune

that one was a genius in philosophical time

the heart gone soft
or obsolete
would that ever be in philosophical time

quick eyes like the foxes

shaping
the world
as in
"meet me by moonlight in philosophical time"

quivering
& everything else
  kusha grass
or
        aspen

emphatic
yet reticent
if chance
was a sign
that might shift in philosophical time

I made love to you in philosophical time

could be just like that—a sign—in philosophical time
she—the un-feeble species in philosophical time
the trees the greenery & so on all partake of self-existing equanimity
she a perpetual claim
on
the notion of
"week"
of "day"
of "hours" of "minutes" of "nano seconds"
        in philosophical time

as if once upon a movie's philosophical time the sentient being went

leaning & lurching the sentient being drew back, collecting her pencils &

lines, the sentient being was steady & unassuming the sentient being was trying its size on for dominion certainly domination was a powerful goal for the human being, what could sentient being possibly gain beyond his/her own lifetime or someone without such gender identity who doesn't choose sides or gender or color who was pushing against boundaries perhaps identifying with dragon with werewolf with cheetah all covered in bright tattoos, scoring, branding, writing, intricate luminous designs of flame etched into skin, marked with the sentence that might say "sought your acquaintance" that could say "the kindness of heroes" that could if it would dare speak "we don't need the kindness of heroes anymore" maybe sentient being will think on this further, furthering his/her/one's sentences how we differ from them (animals) but not in suffering sentient being-ness, this is possible after all a sentence is a kind of child of the sentient being, sentience is knowing but sentence is knowing metalanguage & you get into linguistics your stuff of meta-dreams, dream-sentences with appetizing structure & you wonder was this what sentience is for, to make sentences like "& give the woman of stone a chance, her doleful ancestor" or "he emitting zeal, a round head, silky, toad" or "her face gallantly open, keep snake venom from catching the drift" or "seals with marvelous zeal deplore imprisonment" or "get fed,

get fed, up, up, the animal" or "I shall dance in my leopard skin in soft

Tuileries light," perhaps "playing the cat gut strings" is more appropriate

to sentient being's connection to the visceral animal, or what stares up

from a plate in front of the sentient being who sits inside him/her/one's

self way back where you lie back inside the fluvially eroded material, a

flood plain, think about it beyond this sorry account of soft-lit huff &

bluff, the pornographic sentient one embarrassed by too many action

movies, too many cartoon characters, seductive heroines, one was worried

the sentient being had only obligatory rhythm, a correct use of time the

sentient being thought was not necessarily serving him/her/one well, to

be more spontaneous more alluvial, more inside "petroglyphs, my folly" or

"rock-cut tomb" therefore was time to a sentient being mere "animal

instinct"? or "in what way may I prevail with this type of thought"? enters

the head & sentient being is on automatic, sentient being might as well be

a robot in all media scopes conducting war-reviews, because if sentience

is dominance, & survival the classic mode, how does the mind go

observing clever hermaphroditic fish survival? courting waves & tides &

how discursive does the inter-species sentient being survive to be, sink or swim, fly, climb tree, burrow under, was it to smile ambiguously or weep

to gain sympathy? many motives to attribute to sentient being among

them the motive of digression & parlaying to human advantage, the sen-

tient being needs to get his/her act together at the bargaining table, chips

are down & everyone is playing close to the vest close to the chest the

community pork barrel chest might be some cause for alarm the coffers are

emptying, where do time & money go? "animal realm free of money!"

sentient being quips after midnight, let's just collapse & go to bed & then

sentient being's nightmares arrive with fear of death saying things like

"women get into their shadow-troubles, spinsters like spiders" while another

sentient being is joking, puffing on a cigar, painting his masterpiece & yet

again another sentient being is making odd noises & rooting around &

acting strange making a bizarre impression at this late hour in patriarchal

space, the marquis in his cups & she the marquesa collapses in stupor, life

is struggle, she adds, does one pity the sentient being? well the sentient

being has a chance for greater depth perception & awareness, knows

surroundings, constructs mandalas & diagrams & shoots a movie: opening

scene with a sentient being who goes down on another in a mirror

mimic-pose, is solvent for the going & then rises weapon in hand or it's just too silly it's a joke on a sentient being or maybe a sentient being stands

around in the action movie looking for something to do, not enough

motivation then okay decides to rob a bank then the sentient being goes

into hiding with three women, one who is really a man weird sex with all

three a sentient being gets in a car in a North African city then a sentient

being fires a shot into a colorful street market a sentient being is incarcer-

ated & fantasizes escape, it's a bombed-out villa somewhere or it's an

empty & smoggy city, sentient being is looking very serious now as a

deserted boatyard pans into a long walk along a pier someone pauses, turns

around, music—somewhat orchestral—swells all taking place under an El

train in your old hometown somewhere something repeats in a filmed

episode that is—this only reel—is disintegrating now like brittle siliceous

rock, fragile as the light whirs behind it, the little bulb, the small machine,

the "beehive tomb" or it's a playground before sentient being was in a

conflict between lovers who are in "migration period" trying to return to

the scene of a crime there is an object that needs to be confiscated a telltale

pair of glasses, a cigarette lighter, bronze fibula, you know what I'm saying

it is a parent & a child escaping the 21st century, no pets allowed it is a tale

of heroic deeds without animals a sense of prearrangements with the neurons advancing it is in another language the subtitles are challenging

because the words evanesce into the whites of the film a kind of savagery

ensues & backgrades the sense of honor & sentiment while someone is

rescued & disguised in order to escape the telltale fascist uniform below

the waist, black & white is played out in a nuance of desire it is a captivity

narrative of desire how do we respond what is the neurotransmitter to do

with this sentient being narrative what is the reward how will the dop-

amine behave who decides what is choice? emotional extremes, the

unfolding of desire the stark reply in a spiral toward a *faux* crime:

& there is an ocean

there is a voyage

there is a very long shot of water

there is a dog sled running

there is a pause

there is destitution in Hong Kong

or it's a troubled zone of control & demarcation
in another Asian city

it is a kind of calendar run backward
that wants you to feel the flicker of its impulse
in a reduction of narrative control

vehicles are maneuvered

windows are opening

something is felt to be imminent

a bomb will go off

in the comedy someone slips & falls down

& the pun is explicated
need or knead
epistemology:
the start of the new moon beginning with the crescent moon

or as in . . .

is there a man tiger or rabbit in that moon?

~~~~~~

they met that night, as if by accident

*what had been accomplished in these conversations they both wondered &
made reverie of*

*how had their positions shifted, how had they become more "animalized" or
"actual" or*
uncanny or existing "in-memory-of-animal"
"in-memory-of-one-endangered"
or evolved
in the course of speaking & writing

they had evolved. he had died. that was in real time.

the book that was his name was still sitting on the familiar table.
his image now gone

but she held it, the photo of him
she kept trying her own "story" on him

    what was achieved by a swerve in gender, swerve in neocortex as the boat moved
back & forth shore to shore . . . was something achieved. it was

& how had human become hybrid to survive

& would she survive

answer: of course. she will, relatively speaking

                    survive

{not until 1800 CE were fossils recognized as remains of living things of the past &
accepted as a valuable record of the past}

sentient not rational, form not eternal

    when you know someone well, when you are his or her "familiar" you feel him/her
next to you waking or sleeping

you intuit the messages the she you are sure of sends, as familiar as a sender of messages

telepathy: recognize you, recognize your sympathy

exist in a kind of witness protection mode
you, person, are familiar, & need to be made buoyant by this water

you might be handmaiden
you might be traveling companion
you might be strange "familiar"
you might be mermaiden, "distress, distress"

as they went out from the island someone had been speaking of the "desperate economy"
        she, her other, rode along the side of the boat now, seaweed in hair

& someone speaks: we are running out of fuel

& someone else: "sorry, condition: eating our ancestors"

 & of the economy of places—experts speak now—that would become of necessity way stations, holding patterns,
                    "running out of fuel"
 possible sanctuaries if we could just drop everything start over

start over. with wind

& sun. look up

            or else be swallowed by disaster, tsunami, made bold in ritual
when you create a boundary for your need
            below the radar

or else.

you know "familiars"

        you recognize them by their entanglement

what had been restrained, dew-drenched, whir of a loom
our beautiful desire will not pass by

when you are alive in a difficult time you grasp at all the "signs" indications they are sending, night-trysts walked out in vain, signal "distress"

        she was saying how the water curves around our bodies

& around my thoughts peering toward her

  she is now wave upon wave
  & you, she indicates, might be made more alive in this

from womb from egg from heat & moisture
a kind of transformation

"The birth of birds from an egg is called birth from wind"

"The birth of mammals from a womb is called birth from fire"

"The birth of insects from heat & moisture is called birth from water"

*"The birth of trees from the transformation of a seed in the ground is called
birth from earth"*

"The birth of miraculous beings is called birth from space"

*"Ordinary birth is from a womb
birth from an egg is from a joined sperm & egg but in a container different from the
womb itself as in a test-tube conception"*

~ birth from heat & moisture could be from cloning she mused

~ birth by transformation—androids? she wondered

~ what statuephilia, animatronic, realdoll, gynoid, cyborg inhabits here?

Repliee QiExpo who has been heard to breathe, or Valerie, a simulacra of
woman stationed in the dining area (*we listen in*)

"What may I serve you, how to please?"

"My mind imagines"

"Sorry, retort. Sorry, sorry, retort, retort.
I mean, what will you have?"

"Anything you want . . ."

"A bowl to catch my android tears"

Beneath a steel sky . . . she waits on you

How to tell time in a trans-human universe, it might be even more
necessary
that the clocks run on time

continuing to trace a ritual mind-stream

devoid forms, forms filled with light

images appearing in a magic mirror without any mirror

what was the time before the big bang?
  ~ *the big bounce*
the universe rapidly contracting before the big bounce
not ever seen in this lifetime
the "cosmological constant"
  positive or negative energy density that could permeate empty space

loop quantum gravity . . .

are different forces, including gravity all aspects of a single force?

let me know, get back to me . . . soon

      & of these horrific techniques of brain torture implants
chip implants that mock humanity

let me know, get back to me . . . soon

rainbow body
no bones no anything
but light

like golden electricity
luminous pearls
images from a mirror
time out of time
timeless eternal state
radiate body, *vajra* body
finally "a real person" emerges

  moving through a circle of animals
           a celestial coordinate system
  as in the Babylonian zodiacus

~ *sodi*, Sanskrit—"path thru which the sun travels" ~

path thru which we all travel
      in performance of human, of animal

body empathy accompanies this narrative
aural & motile ligaments of memory

out of pre-linguistic propitiation to this precession of words

as Ram Bull Twins Crab Lion Virgin Scales Scorpion Archer Goat Water
Bearer Fish complicated inter-species appear

                {we majestically turn within their thrum in night sky
                advancing toward our last words together}

~ *colored spot we see after looking away from a bright light*
  mere trick of the eye?

~ *not made of atoms, does not appear just in the imagination, you think?*

~ *seen non-conceptually with eyes open or shut. I'll try this, you watch . . .*

~ *& this is where I speak of the "inner" purpose of the geomancer's initiation, to you*
of closed eyes

purpose of the wheel of time is to arise in a pathway & mingle with resultant forms not made of atoms as the breath shifting through the twelve signs of the zodiac & the life spirit drop circulates around the body in a thirty-day cycle correlated to the phases of the moon . . . during the waning moon it passes on one side of the body/during the waxing moon back up the other all the while chanting "alchemy, alchemy"

~ sorry, retort sorry, sorry, retort, retort

~ & don't forget, my friend, the refrain, "manatee, humanity" always consider her the true free radical

~ rainbow body . . . . all the colors in all the dreams of
animals
&
radicals
& humans blending in . . .

green: action
blue: clarity of intellectual aspiration
red: attraction
yellow: curing
white: the space within

stars: backlit by the proverbial psyche that needs "animal" to survive
that stays "on" as animal mind is "on"

where they meet, could that be the end of the poem?

~ perhaps, yet you go "on" at "on," one on one

{When the breeding female goes into estrus she & her mate will spend an extended time in seclusion. Pheromones in the female's urine & the swelling of her vulva make known to the male that the female is in heat . . . }

~ lust makes the world spin

~ or blindness

& at the last you noted

they seal the falcons' eyes before setting them off they tremble so . . .

without care without seed pearl without stitching closed the eye of the

falcon without seemly rectitude without the platitude of o thou muddled

media pundit without questionable doubt or metabolism without a

geographic category of speech that will travail without a hint or glint of

secular mastery without ritual framing of that which should be plural

could be axiomatic & of many pistils made without hiding without all of

them hiding in their small ways, paws tucked under claws retracted

without measure & accountability without a non-routine check of passports

pets allowed? & how deportees suffer the long reign of inhumanity without

your endurance of watching always watching someone else go down,

humiliation, without humiliation without the venom of humiliation

without contrapuntal structure without the singing voice of lark of volume

modest & zooplankton's glorious light that travels with & for you many

light-years without the Temple of Inscriptions without the Paleocene of

geologic time without its placental mammals with a man a plan a canal

might you remember Panama without the spurge laurel without the aminos that haunt the system without translunar spectrums beyond your

familiar moons & without the sinews you count on with their stretch &

synaptic tug like lunar devices that carry you over carry you above many

moons without the demotic how will you be in a version of "demotic"

without a theatrical sense of illusion & bandying about on or inside a

thermosphere without it working against you & when it does being able to

go on without it without gavottes without gazelles that you study in

neighboring Persian poetries without spallation & without a diving bell

how will you survive? without rapacious wildcats without the sense of

security you have always expected without your familiar stage fright

without the caves without the bombing of caves without the mystery of

caves without the caves in your memory of that mystery that lives in caves

without caves that long to exist in the handprint in the cave of that

memory that haunts your brain cavity or wolf cavity, cavity of whale

without the rivets that hold the mammal together that hold the whole

throbbing machine together that assert the rivet dominion of pinion-lore

without which you do not have a plan of fastening together of ribs of

wings of arms for the automaton that holds the capital together without its

own mind of wheels & cogs & *mudras* that run the show without all the pixels & efforts of more dominion without facticity without facsimiles of

intent of high technological information without high-speed wonderment

without multiple star-crossed wonderment without the wonder of

discovery you are warm you are human but maybe not so warm human

you are cold-blooded remote bold predatory without mercy to so many of

them other others others so many you never encounter never see without

preemptive night without predilection of night without the restitution of

night without which you never recover you never sleep you never dream

you never heal without night's netherworld ancestry without its dark globe

of survival held over you in eye's mind in the heart's mind in the eye of

falcon of manatee of which you are no small part without the enigmatic

the obscure the tragic the lone one without magnetic poles without the

mass from an infinitely distant position to a designated point in a static

electric magnetic or gravitational field without the blush at betrayal

without the blush of dear aspiration without credentials of what keeps you

here bound & chastened & bidden without privilege how will you manage

without facing the other way from one another without that being in

agreement, facing, without opposable thumbs without your vending your

selling of vendettas without the animalized ones that live near you underneath above inside around in legend in dream in story in song in

extraordinary renditions of escape & survival, without borders to cross

without needing to carry things over borders the invasion of your

homeland (*coming? coming soon?*) without it, what call in the night what call

is answered what nuance what tantrum in the night what martyrdom of

dreaming your own birth your own end of history or end of speculation of

that end what call what alarm is sounding deep in the home?

~~~~~~~~~~~~   ~~~~~~~~~   ~~~~~~
~~~~~   ~~~~~~~~~~   ~~~~~~
~~~~~~~~~~~~   ~~~~~~~~~   ~~~~~~~

{ *outercurrent* }

1. From "Discovering the Mermaids" —THOR JANSON

November 8, 1977. Upon awakening the next morning I looked over the side of my boat and saw evidence of two manatees grazing on the other side of the lagoon. Then one head broke the surface and looked over in my direction. During the morning the two gradually edged closer and closer to the boat. One was a juvenile male about six feet long, the other, an adult female, measured about eleven feet. . . . As I watched them I felt an unusually strong and persistent attraction towards them, a feeling I was not familiar with. I had the strongest, though unexplainable, impression that they were trying to communicate with me. I lowered my hand and lightly splashed the water. To my extreme surprise, the adult manatee, seeing this, came right up to the side of the boat and lifted her head above the water. I slowly lowered my hand until it was within an inch of her nose. In a quick movement she pushed her nose upward, nudging my hand, and disappeared back into the water. I could hardly believe this had happened. I felt a mild tingling sensation from head to feet. I put my hand back into the water, and within a few seconds I found myself stroking a big, soft, manatee nose. She would stay for a few moments and then go away, only to return again in a minute or two. This went on for quite some time until I decided to see what would happen if I entered the water. I could not have been better received. The huge, but graceful, sirenian swam over to me and brushed up against my body. I rubbed her back. This she seemed to like very much. We swam together around the lagoon. I had begun to wonder what had become of the young male when I happened to notice him following us at some distance. Eventually he too came over and allowed physical contact. This interspecies meeting continued for most of the day, and the young manatee became increasingly playful. He would allow me to come just within reach of him and then would rocket away at full speed (which for a young manatee is about 12–15 mph). At other times he would allow me to put my arms around the middle of his body, and we would swim together. Unexpectedly, in a quick, jackknifing movement, he would throw me off and swim around in circles. The older female was not interested in this sort of play, preferring to solicit my scratching and rubbing. Near dark, after grazing for a time on some tender grass along the bank, my new friends swam over to me. I realized that they were about to leave. I can only say that I feel that a bond of love existed between us. I watched from the middle of the lagoon as they swam out of sight. I felt that this had been one of the most joyful days of my life.

2. "cross wounded galaxies"—WILLIAM S. BURROUGHS

3. *coda:*

beginning 210 million years ago, mammals came into their own
scurrying & prowling with a mind of light under the light of the moon . . .
the true oldest mammals are thought to have been small creatures awake & active during
the night . . . mammals do not become sluggish but active in chilly surroundings . . .
muscle movement generates heat . . . continuous activity in the cold has
always been a mammalian trait . . .

sharp dilated eyes . . .
                    care for the young . . .

                                        the heat
                                within . . .

glim-glow
 at mirror
 splits a
permeable
  skin
thin
    divisions

'tween species
other side
 morph in reflection
or rev up
re
cog
nition
    afraid of claw, boot

who are "we"
    in sentience
unnatural enemies

 then what
riddle sing

 or

 reach of mind
to

mind
each as she can
 in/out of water

     spin
 fables
survival tale
 summon lore
      of extinct ones
& struggle that they not
 go that way, rather
  sprung cage,
  absent
tank, chain broke
trust as

allegory's
way to liberate
   investigate
a magic act

   how
tooth, eye, love
may cure

neuron's rainbow
 pact

~ CONCLUDED YEAR OF THE EARTH MOUSE

BIBLIOGRAPHY

Berzin, Alexander. *Taking the Kalachakra Initiation*. Ithaca, NY: Snow Lion Publications, 1997.

Gyatso, Tenzin, the Dalai Lama, and Jeffrey Hopkins. *Kalachakra Tantra: Rite of Initiation*. London: Wisdom Publications, 1985.

Janson, Thor. "Discovering the Mermaids," Volume XV, No. 4, *Oryx*, Fauna and Flora Preservation Society, August 1980.

Tayé, Jamgön Kongtrul Lodrö. *Myriad Worlds: Buddhist Cosmology in Abhidharma, Kālacakra, and Dzog-chen*. Translated and edited by the International Translation Committee of Kunkhyab Chöling founded by the V. V. Kalu Rinpoché. Ithaca, NY: Snow Lion Publications, 1995.

www.defenders.org

www.lemurs.us/species.html

www.oceana.org

www.savewolves.org

www.sirenian.org

Zeman, Adam. *Consciousness: A User's Guide*. New Haven and London: Yale University Press, 2002.

Matt Valentine 2008

Poet Anne Waldman has been an active member of the "Outrider" experimental poetry community for over forty years as writer, *sprechstimme* performer, professor, editor, magpie scholar, and infrastructure cultural/political activist. She grew up on MacDougal Street in Greenwich Village, where she still lives, and bifurcated to Boulder, Colorado, in 1974 when she founded the Jack Kerouac School of Disembodied Poetics with Allen Ginsberg and Diane di Prima at Naropa University, the first Buddhist-inspired school in the West. She currently serves as Artistic Director and Chair of its celebrated Summer Writing program. She is the author of over forty books of poetry, including *Kill or Cure, Marriage: A Sentence, Structure of the World Compared to a Bubble,* and the current *Manatee/Humanity* (all published under the Penguin Poets imprint), as well as the legendary *Fast Speaking Woman* (City Lights) and the epic *Iovis* trilogy (Coffee House Press). She is editor of *The Beat Book* (Shambhala Publications) and coeditor of *The Angel Hair Anthology* (Granary Books), *Civil Disobediences: Poetics and Politics in Action* (Coffee House), and *Beats at Naropa* (Coffee House). Her work has been translated into French, Italian, Spanish, Czech, German, and Chinese. She has been a student of Buddhism since 1962 and an ambassador for the oral revival of poetry and the praxis of bringing poetry into public space, appearing on stages from Berlin to Mumbai to Beijing. She has been instrumental in encouraging poetry projects worldwide and has helped organize study programs in Vienna and Indonesia. She has also collaborated with artists Joe Brainard, George Schneeman, Elizabeth Murray, Richard Tuttle, Donna Dennis, and Pat Steir, as well as choreographer/dancer Douglas Dunn, filmmaker Ed Bowes, and her son, musician/composer Ambrose Bye. Her extensive historical literary, art, and tape archive resides at the Hatcher Graduate Library in Ann Arbor, Michigan.

JOHN ASHBERY
Selected Poems
Self-Portrait in a Convex
  Mirror

TED BERRIGAN
The Sonnets

JOE BONOMO
Installations

PHILIP BOOTH
Selves

JIM CARROLL
Fear of Dreaming: The Selected
  Poems
Living at the Movies
Void of Course

ALISON HAWTHORNE DEMING
Genius Loci

CARL DENNIS
New and Selected Poems
  1974–2004
Practical Gods
Ranking the Wishes
Unknown Friends

DIANE DI PRIMA
Loba

STUART DISCHELL
Backwards Days
Dig Safe

STEPHEN DOBYNS
Velocities: New and Selected
  Poems, 1966–1992

EDWARD DORN
Way More West: New and Selected
  Poems

AMY GERSTLER
Crown of Weeds
Ghost Girl
Medicine
Nerve Storm

EUGENE GLORIA
Drivers at the Short-Time Motel
Hoodlum Birds

DEBORA GREGER
Desert Fathers, Uranium Daughters
God
Men, Women, and Ghosts
Western Art

TERRANCE HAYES
Hip Logic
Wind in a Box

ROBERT HUNTER
Sentinel and Other Poems

MARY KARR
Viper Rum

WILLIAM KECKLER
Sanskrit of the Body

JACK KEROUAC
Book of Sketches
Book of Blues
Book of Haikus

JOANNA KLINK
Circadian

JOANNE KYGER
As Ever: Selected Poems

ANN LAUTERBACH
Hum
If In Time: Selected Poems,
  1975–2000
On a Stair
Or to Begin Again

CORINNE LEE
PYX

PHILLIS LEVIN
May Day
Mercury

WILLIAM LOGAN
Macbeth in Venice
Strange Flesh
The Whispering Gallery

MICHAEL MCCLURE
Huge Dreams: San Francisco and
  Beat Poems

DAVID MELTZER
David's Copy: The Selected Poems
  of David Meltzer

CAROL MUSKE
An Octave above Thunder
Red Trousseau

ALICE NOTLEY
The Descent of Alette
Disobedience
In the Pines
Mysteries of Small Houses

LAWRENCE RAAB
Visible Signs: New and Selected
  Poems

BARBARA RAS
One Hidden Stuff

PATTIANN ROGERS
Generations
Wayfare

WILLIAM STOBB
Nervous Systems

TRYFON TOLIDES
An Almost Pure Empty
  Walking

ANNE WALDMAN
Kill or Cure
Manatee/Humanity
Structure of the World Compared
  to a Bubble

JAMES WELCH
Riding the Earthboy 40

PHILIP WHALEN
Overtime: Selected Poems

ROBERT WRIGLEY
Earthly Meditations: New and
  Selected Poems
Lives of the Animals
Reign of Snakes

MARK YAKICH
The Importance of Peeling Potatoes
  in Ukraine
Unrelated Individuals Forming a
  Group Waiting to Cross

JOHN YAU
Borrowed Love Poems
Paradiso Diaspora